"*Handbook for a Post*-Roe *America* is the survival guide American women will need to carry around like a Bible if we'll ever survive the GOP's rigid rule over US—er, the US. . . . everything a pro-choice woman needs to know about *Roe*, including what'll make it go away, how to resist, and what to do if she gets pregnant while abortion's either completely or nearly illegal."
—CRYSTAL ERICKSON, *Bust*

"In *Handbook for a Post*-Roe *America*, Marty walks readers through the various futures of abortion rights in the U.S. and provides advice on how to plan ahead."
—MELISSA JELTSEN, *Huffington Post*

"*Handbook* is a road map toward an uncertain future, offering not only proactive measures that advocates can take to protect abortion access, but also insight into how to stay on the offensive when it comes to anti-choicers. Marty's extensive background on the topic makes this book a critical read for anyone new to abortion politics; those who have been in the fight, meanwhile, will find specifics and helpful tools to share with other advocates. Whether it's figuring out how to protect ourselves online, or navigating what kind of reactive activism is most productive (spoiler: it's not counterprotesting at clinics), readers will find an accessible guide for all abortion-advocacy levels."
—CAROLINE REILLY, Bitch Media

"Invaluable information useful both for an individual woman seeking an abortion and for those seeking to politically organize and fight the injustices of the anti-abortionists."
—DAVID ROSEN, CounterPunch

"A necessary primer on organizing, fundraising, and avoiding legal trouble when and if you must break an unconstitutional law."
—*Bustle*

NEW HANDBOOK
FOR A
POST-*ROE*
AMERICA

The Complete Guide to Abortion Legality, Access, and Practical Support

ROBIN MARTY

introduction by
AMANDA PALMER

Seven Stories Press
New York • Oakland • London

Seven Stories Press
140 Watt Street
New York, NY 10013
www.sevenstories.com

Library of Congress Cataloging-in-Publication Data

Names: Marty, Robin, author.
Title: New handbook for a post-Roe America / Robin Marty.
Description: Second edition | New York, NY : Seven Stories Press, [2021] | Includes bibliographical references and index.
Identifiers: LCCN 2020055647 (print) | LCCN 2020055648 (ebook) | ISBN 9781644210581 (trade paperback) | ISBN 9781644210598 (ebook)
Subjects: LCSH: Reproductive rights--United States--History. | Abortion--United States--History. | Abortion--Law and legislation--United States--History. | Pro life movement--United States--History. | Pro-choice movement--United States--History. | Social change--United States.
Classification: LCC HQ767 .M385 2021 (print) | LCC HQ767 (ebook) | DDC 362.1988/800973--dc23
LC record available at https://lccn.loc.gov/2020055647
LC ebook record available at https://lccn.loc.gov/2020055648

Book design by Jon Gilbert

Printed in the USA.

9 8 7 6 5 4 3 2 1

Contents

Introduction

Hi, my name is Amanda, and for the next few minutes, consider me your friend. Then you can get to the practical parts of the book that you actually need.

Chances are good that if you're opening up this book, you may be pregnant and about to deal with an abortion. Or you have a friend, partner, or family member who's in the thick of it.

Guess what? Nobody—I mean nobody—really wants to talk about this stuff. Nobody really wants to write a book about it, either, or sing about it, or make art about it. It's just too uncomfortable and awkward.

That's why Robin Marty, the author of this book, deserves extra special credit. She could have written about just about anything else and had an easier life.

I'm a singer/songwriter by trade, and I've had three abortions. Yes. Three.

I had my first abortion at seventeen in Boston; I was a scared kid in my senior year of high school. My second abortion happened in Scotland shortly after getting married in my thirties and finding out that, aside from the fact that the pregnancy was accidental, the fetus wasn't even viable due to an antibiotic I'd taken. And my third abortion—the hardest one—was simply by choice a few years later. I got pregnant and had a breakdown-level existential crisis, struggling with confusion, guilt, and ambivalence for weeks, doing things like googling "what do Buddhists think about abortion" on my phone, hidden under my covers in the middle of the night. I just wanted some time to decide for me. I decided, ultimately, that I wasn't ready. I had an abortion in New York.

The abortions all had one thing in common: they were easy to access, immediately, and they were safe and legal. I was a teenager with well-off, liberal parents, and later, I was a well-off person in countries where I never gave a thought to the legality of abortion, or the expense. I know that is a privilege not available to countless others.

This is a practical handbook about abortion. It's a very direct—and sadly necessary—collection of tools, facts, resources, and information in an era of American history that's gone very dark in the area of reproductive rights. But I've always felt there was a second handbook needed when dealing with abortion, the handbook I wished existed so many times in my life, but couldn't find: an emotional handbook. A handbook about how to navigate the feelings.

I spent the majority of 2019 touring the world, playing a piano on a big theater stage every night, right until COVID-19 hit and cancelled everything. During my show, I looked out at tens of thousands of people sitting in the dark as I told the stories of my three abortions, and also the stories of being pregnant and giving birth, and the story of enduring a miscarriage alone in a hotel room. So fun and entertaining! No, actually, the show was really . . . funny. And sad. And healing. One of the songs was titled "Voicemail for Jill," which felt less like a song and more like a prayer, and a code that I'd cracked after a lifetime of tackling the seemingly impossible task of writing about abortion in a song without clouding it in humor and irony.

In it, I sing:

You don't need to offer the right explanation,
You don't need to beg for redemption or ask for forgiveness.
And you don't need a courtroom inside of your head
Where you're acting as judge and accused and defendant
    and witness.

One of the biggest difficulties of experiencing an abortion is that you have to deal with several roiling and complicated feelings, in real time.

There's the way *you* feel about *your* abortion, anywhere on the scale from "it's not a big deal, truly" to "this is the end of the whole goddamn world." All those spots on the emotional spectrum are valid; you're feeling what you're feeling. But then there's the extra feeling you have to carry about what The World may be feeling about your abortion.

What your parents would think, what the other party involved in the pregnancy would think (or would think if they knew), what your partner thinks (or would think if they knew), what your children would think, what the church would think, what God would think, what Goddess would think, what your dog or cat would think . . . I mean . . . when you're pregnant and heading for an abortion, it gets weird. The entire landscape around you can look like a giant wall of impenetrable judgment. Pretty much everybody has an opinion about abortion. And if you're having one, that probably means—in your anxious head—that everybody's got an opinion about YOU, and your decision. And, you, my friend, do not need that extra burden right now. Not when you're already dealing with an abortion and the logistics and physical pain of the thing itself. It is maddening, it is confusing, and most of all, it is isolating.

Dealing emotionally with an abortion is like trying to walk across a balance beam while carrying a pile of logs in your arms. Blindfolded. You must move forward. Time will not stop for you. But, more often than not, the room is empty, nobody is cheering for your success, nobody is coming to your aid, nobody is offering words of joyful encouragement. Help is not on the way.

That is why I am so glad you are holding this book. This book *is* help. And this book is here to remind you that you are not alone.

No matter what your situation is, where you are, who you are, or what you're going through, I want to personally reach through the pages, give you a hug, and hold your hand. What you're dealing with may be a very easy decision, or a very fraught and complicated one, but either way, you're living in a culture that is not built to support you, to hold you, to nurture you, and make an abortion a simple, practical, calm, and drama-free process. Even if abortion stays legal in America, we still live in a culture that, for the most part, expects you to deal with your abortion as a clandestine operation, sweeping the event away from your life as if it never happened.

Abortion is a silent and shame-wrapped footnote in the lives of millions and millions of people.

Abortion can be *lonely*. So incredibly lonely.

Many years ago, in America, I was invited over to a family's house for the Christmas holidays. As an endlessly touring musician, I was used to getting generous invitations into people's homes, and one of my greatest pleasures in life is the strange flash intimacy that occurs when you're suddenly thrust into a holiday home with near-total strangers. The invitation had come through my friendship with a man—let's call him Piotr—and he'd confided in me a week before that his daughter—let's call her Janey—had just had an abortion. Janey was twenty-five, living with her boyfriend, and had considered the idea of having the baby for about three days before deciding it was just not the right time: she was broke, she was young, the relationship was too new, there were lots of reasons.

There was a collection of ten or twelve other relatives at this weekend-long Christmas gathering. As we broke bread and went for walks, everything was discussed: politics, different family Christmas traditions, the food and shopping plans, our life stories. Janey's abortion was not a topic of discussion, and I had no idea if anyone else in the family knew what had happened days before. But as cake was passed around, and presents were opened, and games were played, I did find myself noticing that Janey was withdrawn, moving about gingerly, and she and her boyfriend said very little. I wondered who knew. The various family members followed a rainbow of faiths; one was a lifelong Hare Krishna, one had converted to Judaism, most of these folks had been raised Christian but weren't practicing. They were a liberal family. I can't imagine that anyone there was anti-abortion. But I didn't know. Janey and her boyfriend seemed to leave the gathering as early as was politely possible.

The crazy-making thing about having an abortion is that it's just not okay to talk about it in the way we talk about . . . anything else. Even discussing miscarriage is much more socially acceptable. There's really no simpler way to put it: it's just not something people want to talk about, it's not something people want to think about, and it's not something people want to have to imagine. And no wonder. In America, so much drama and weight has been foisted onto the topic that it's almost always easier—even if you're an outspoken, confident, self-possessed person—to say nothing. Why rock the boat?

I have two Facebook pages: a public musician one, where I talk about abortion rights frequently, and a "friends and family" page that's more private and followed by a few hundred people, instead of thousands. I never post about abortion rights, or discuss my abortion politics, on that page. Why? There's always that *one* distant cousin I worry about. I don't want to be the annoying one. I don't want to ruffle feathers within my wider family. I don't want to offend, or disturb the peace.

But the very worst thing about not talking about abortion is this: it perpetuates a cultural catastrophe. When you get an abortion, there is no open community support, there are few rituals, there is no space in this culture for healing. You are generally just lonely.

If Janey had come into Christmas dinner with a fresh cast on her broken leg, or a scarf on her head from her first round of chemo, there would have been sympathy, concern, and freely offered help and assistance. She'd have lain on the couch while we all brought her tea and cake and told her to please take it easy for goodness' sake.

But she'd been through an abortion, and whether or not everybody in that room knew, this sort of treatment was not in the cards. I imagine Janey shuffling off to the bathroom, dealing with soaked sanitary pads, taking deep breaths and feeling totally disconnected from the chitchat in the room. No wonder she wanted to get out of there so quickly.

But abortion does not have to be lonely.

As Robin points out in this book, the Internet can be your friend when it comes to not feeling alone. I found a Facebook group called "Heart Healing After Abortion" that gave me an incredible amount of comfort as I lurked and scrolled through hundreds of posts about mixed feelings, waves of relief mixed with waves of grief, and other super-personal stories.

I didn't need to post there to feel validated. What I really wanted was to *not feel lonely.*

A few years later, when I finally got off the fence and decided to have a child, I had an experience that I wouldn't wish on my worst enemy. I was three months pregnant, resolved and happy about it, and I was about to tell the big, wide world. I'd had some routine blood tests. I'd asked the doctor's office not to reveal the sex of the baby, I wanted to be surprised. I was alone at a friend's house—my partner was overseas—when a phone call came in. A female nurse on the other side of the phone said:

"Is this Amanda Palmer?"

"Yes . . . ?"

"Hello. I have some information for you. First of all, it's a boy. And you've tested positive for a very rare chromosomal defect. Fifty percent of the people who test positive for this deformity choose to abort. We need to discuss next steps."

My stomach dropped. I was being told by a total stranger, over the phone, that I was carrying a fetus that was—at best—going to be born sterile, and—at worst—going to have severe physical abnormalities, and, in the worst of all cases, might not even survive the first few years of life. She told me to come in for a follow-up test to confirm the results.

The oxygen drained out of my body as I walked to my bedroom, almost unable to breathe, and I lay down and screamed a blood-curdling animal scream, at the top of my lungs, into a pillow.

You are being punished, I thought to myself. *This is what you get for being so uncertain. This is what you get for having three abortions. This is what you get.*

For about a week, I barely left that room and I lived in a circle of hell. I furiously and obsessively googled information about the deformity. I imagined my life, this child's life. The choice was clear: have a fourth abortion, or gamble with bringing this potentially disabled child into the world. I went in for a second test to confirm the results, and a few days later, the phone rang. A new stranger on the line told me:

"Sorry! Good news. That earlier test was a false positive. Your baby is perfectly healthy!"

You should have heard the agonizing moan-scream of relief that escaped my mouth when I hung up the phone; another animal sound I'd never heard come out of me.

That was about six years ago, and relief has graduated to horror when I think about that story. Not only the lack of humanity shown in those phone calls, but . . . what would have I done? Kept the baby? Had another abortion?

I'll never know, because I was lucky. I didn't have to make the choice. And if I'd made the choice to abort, it would have been legal and easy.

That harrowing moment in my life made me realize I had to speak up at every possible moment about how critical it is to protect the human rights of pregnant people. Your body, your choice. The end.

I once had a yoga teacher who had a saying he would haul out when we were about to do some very difficult and strenuous pose: "If you can, you must." Yes, it's hard and annoying. No, you don't really want to. And it took me years—decades—to get comfortable with the idea of telling these stories. Even after the seventieth stage show last year, I still felt a twinge of discomfort in the pit of my stomach as I told the story of what it felt like to have my feet up in the stirrups. I always cringed inside, and I even cringe a bit now writing this. What if someone out there HATES me for saying this stuff? Someone surely does. I need to say it anyway.

At the same time, the more I say it, the less pain and power it holds. Like water over a stone, I've started to wear down the calcified, leftover traces of shame that were always lurking around in the back rooms of my head.

Until recently, in Ireland, if you had an abortion, administered an abortion, or even had knowledge about an "illicit" abortion, you could go to jail. An entire country swore itself to secrecy when it came to the topic of abortion. I'm thinking right now of the thousands of people who fought for abortion to become decriminalized in Ireland, and then northern Ireland. And more recently, all the people who fought for the same rights, and won them, in Argentina.

I'm thinking of the hundreds of people who found me after my show last year, whispering "I've never told anyone . . ." and going on to tell me about abortions they'd experienced ten, twenty, or thirty years before.

Or the one they'd had last week. Or the one they were taking their partner to get in a few days. I was so overwhelmed by the sheer number of people keeping the truth under wraps.

I'm thinking about the college student I met a few years ago—we were having wine in a bar after a rehearsal together—who told me she could forgive herself the first abortion she had at seventeen, but not the second one she had a year later when she was eighteen.

I'm thinking about my friend who's a mother of four. She had an abortion recently after deciding that she just couldn't handle another child. She kept it secret from her family.

I'm thinking about how I was never alone, and just didn't know it.

I'm thinking about my song again.

You don't need to offer the right explanation,
You don't need to beg for redemption or ask for forgiveness.
And you don't need a courtroom inside of your head
Where you're acting as judge and accused and defendant
and witness.

You may be about to be a person with a story. A person with a story about an abortion.

You may not ever be able to tell it publicly, for any number of reasons. If you cannot tell your story because it's just too complicated or dangerous, don't. Stay safe. Protect yourself. But if you *can?* Your story, if told, will leave the door propped wide open behind you, so that someone else will not feel so alone. Don't forget . . . whoever is behind you: they need you.

They need you.

Reach back, shed your shame, and tell your story.

If you can, you must.

Amanda Palmer
Aotearoa New Zealand
January 2021

Prologue

Why This Second Edition? (2020)

When I first wrote the original *Handbook for a Post-*Roe *America* in the summer and fall of 2018, Justice Anthony Kennedy had recently retired from the Supreme Court and been replaced by the ultra-conservative Brett Kavanaugh, President Donald Trump's second appointment in just two years in office. The 2018 midterms were complete and gave Democrats back a majority in the House and control over more state legislatures than at any point since the great Tea Party wave election of 2010 shifted the nation to the right. While the end of *Roe v. Wade* still seemed imminent, the fact that the GOP no longer had a full stranglehold on all three branches of the federal government (and had lost their hold on the governor's office in Michigan, Kansas, Wisconsin, and other states) provided a little bit of breathing room.

Then the 2019 legislative sessions started and all bets were off.

Blue states took the impending likelihood of *Roe* being overturned as a wake-up call to codify abortion rights while they still could, knowing that in the near future they might be responsible not only for providing access in their own states, but also for offering abortion care to patients in conservative states where the procedure would become illegal. Meanwhile, red states began in concert to pass the most restrictive and blatantly unconstitutional state laws opposing abortion that the country had ever seen. Bans on abortion after the first trimester, after the first so-called heartbeat, and even after the simple act of fertilization spread across the South, Midwest, and Rust Belt, many states no longer allowing exceptions if there was a fetal anomaly, a sexual assault, or even a threat to the pregnant patient's health.

The good news, of course, is that none of these bills ever went into effect. They brought awareness to the fragility of the constitutional right to an abortion, they energized a nation of activists, they caused people to donate millions of dollars to organizations to ensure access would be maintained as much as possible in the abortion deserts that already existed in much of the US. But no state was able to make abortion completely illegal, despite how hard they tried.

At least, not until the pandemic hit.

The novel coronavirus was a clear health care catastrophe on its own, but COVID-19 also provided an immediate snapshot of a post-*Roe* landscape without any of the grand pageantry of a Supreme Court ruling. The same states that have vowed to make abortion illegal the moment they are allowed jumped on the opportunity to close abortion clinics within their borders, claiming it a matter of "public health" rather than political opportunism. As abortion providers opened and closed periodically and without warning—some in response to shelter-in-place orders, others shuttered by governors then reopened by judges, then closed again by appeals, and a few simply due to a lack of doctors to staff them—reproductive health activists saw firsthand and in real time just how thin the strands of our support network can become when there is a national crisis.

The surge of anti-abortion legislation since 2019, followed by the COVID-19 pandemic of 2020, exposed the variety of ways advocates and pregnant people will be forced to adapt if abortion is made partially or completely illegal in the United States. It has also exposed a number of places where the first edition of *Handbook for a Post-*Roe *America* failed to anticipate what would be needed if legal abortion clinics truly ceased to exist—a situation that seems even more inevitable with the addition of Amy Coney Barrett, yet another Trump appointed conservative justice, to the Supreme Court in October 2020. There are some events that simply cannot be planned for until they have been experienced firsthand, and a country without legal abortion clinics in every state is one of them.

Hopefully this second edition will fill in all of the gaps left in the previous version and better anticipate this new landscape—because we are already in a post-*Roe* America, even if the Supreme Court has yet to make that ruling final.

Why This Book? (2018)

For a large section of the US population, the 2016 presidential election was a turning point. It shook complacent mainstream Americans out of their stupor and alerted them to the danger that marginalized communities already knew: that as long as the financial and political power of the country remained concentrated in the hands of the rich, the white, the male, and the conservative, those outside that power structure would see their own rights dismantled at a rapid pace.

The realization brought millions to the streets on January 21, 2017, as the Women's March spurred women and their allies in cities throughout the US to protest President Donald Trump's inauguration. In commercial airports, people protested the administration's Muslim travel ban, while white allies joined the community of Standing Rock in their ongoing effort to stop the Dakota Pipeline project. Back in DC the March on Washington protested the lack of gun restrictions after a year full of mass shootings, and all along the border protestors gathered as asylum seekers and their children were ripped from each other's arms and deported simply for the crime of seeking safety in the United States.

It took the reality of a puppet-figure Republican president, a religious right-dominated Congress, and now the most conservative Supreme Court in modern history to finally push progressive Americans of privilege to take action. For cisgender, straight, white, middle- and upper-class women especially, the idea that legal abortion (and even birth control) could actually disappear, and that the restrictions could be vast enough to affect more than just those of color, those in low-population areas and the South, and the rural and urban poor has become a harsh reality. The announcement that Supreme Court justice Anthony Kennedy was retiring and that yet another Trump nomination would tip the court to the right for decades to come was a wake-up call that has thrown those not regularly engaged in reproductive-rights activism into action.

But what, exactly, should we be doing right now?

While this moment may feel like a crisis point, the truth is that for many communities this fight has been going on for decades, even centuries. Modern gynecology came about through experimentation on Black slaves. Today's contraceptives were initially tested—often coercively and without any informed consent—on women of color. Our medical history is highlighted by periods of sterilization of those who were disabled, or too poor, or the wrong color, or who had what we considered "too many" children. The decades prior to *Roe v. Wade* were filled with young girls hidden away to give birth, only to have their babies stolen and given to "worthier" families.

While *Roe* and the cases that preceded it made birth control and abortion legal, they did nothing to curtail the coercive power our government wields over the bodies of those who can give birth. *Roe* limited abortion only to those who could afford it, while at the same time limiting the types of governmental assistance available to those who wanted to give birth and had larger families but didn't have the financial means. The same government that forbids abortion coverage in Medicaid insurance also allows states to put caps on how many children a mother can receive welfare benefits for. The same states closing abortion clinics and making it hard for the uninsured to access affordable birth control also periodically propose financial incentives for those who are poor to undergo sterilization procedures.[1]

This isn't a crisis the Trump administration caused. This is only a crisis that Trump has brought to the main stage, one that he has finally forced us all to acknowledge and motivated us all to fight—even those who until now thought abortion either a settled issue or one that didn't affect them directly.

Now, the question is how to organize, and how to do it without replicating efforts, without undermining the work that has gone on for generations, and without putting others in danger. This book is written primarily for those who are looking at ways to prepare for the worst-case scenarios in a post-*Roe* America—an America where pregnant people may need to travel across state lines, or obtain illegal abortion-inducing medications, or keep their abortions secret from partners, family, and the authorities. It is meant to provide an action plan that will allow you to do the type of activism that you are best suited for—whether it is providing financial support, offering yourself as someone who can protest or work outside the legal system because of the privilege that comes from your wealth, able-bodiedness, race, gender, or geographic location, or working within the political system to undo the oppressive laws that have restricted people's ability to control their own reproductive futures. And it is meant to provide a personal blueprint for dealing with an unplanned pregnancy when abortion may be difficult—if not impossible—to access.

These tactics aren't meant for everyone. They are meant for those who have the privilege to be able to put their time, skills, money, and even personal freedom into making abortion accessible for everyone. Now that we all recognize the threat and are ready to act, we can—and must—finally shoulder this burden together.

Likely

1) A case makes it to the Supreme Court within the next few years that allows the bench to overturn *Roe*, and they do.

   ▪ There are already a number of cases in lower state courts and appeals circuits that could be reviewed at the SCOTUS level, allowing the court to rule on the issue in the very near future. Plus, if a federal twenty-week abortion ban were passed and signed into law, it would immediately be sent to the Supreme Court for review if anyone chose to challenge it.

   ▪ If the court rules that abortion legality should be left to the states to decide through any of these cases, that ends *Roe* and allows the trigger laws (laws on the books in certain states that immediately make abortion illegal if *Roe* is overturned) to go into effect, and opens the door for total bans in other states.

2) The Supreme Court rules that there is still a constitutional right to an abortion, but that the viability standard is outdated and "fetal pain" should be the new standard.

   ▪ If a state or federal twenty-week ban (twenty weeks into pregnancy being the point at which abortion opponents claim a fetus can "feel pain" in the womb, although the vast majority of medical experts disagree with that statement) is heard by the court, the conservatives could rule that "fetal pain" makes a better point in the pregnancy at which a fetus's right to life outweighs the rights of the person carrying it to terminate, undoing the "viability" standard that has been in place since *Roe* but still technically leaving abortion legal.

   ▪ If this happens, anti-abortion policy makers and legislators are prepared to pass bills stating that fetal pain actually begins far earlier in the pregnancy, as early as six weeks' gestation. This will allow states to effectively ban abortion if they choose to, without actually violating the constitutional right to an abortion.

3) States pass any laws they want—but don't actually ban abortion completely—and the Supreme Court lets them.

- There's also the possibility that the court will simply refuse to hear any cases involving abortion whatsoever, going utterly silent on the issue. Because the state and federal judiciaries have been packed with conservative justices, especially since President Donald Trump was elected, states could very easily decide to pass the most restrictive laws they can short of an outright ban, and as long as a federal judge sides with them and the Supreme Court refuses to hear a challenge, they will stay in place.

- In many ways this could be a very appealing scenario for conservative politicians, allowing some states to ban abortion without the potential blowback from voters that would come from putting a full ban in place. If a restriction is so limiting that no clinics are left open, abortion is no longer available in that state even if it is technically legal. If a state bans abortion after a heartbeat can be heard, but clinics will not do a termination before that point because they need to be sure there is enough development visible to ensure it is not ectopic, that ends abortion. All SCOTUS needs to do is refuse to do anything at all.

4) The Supreme Court rules that there is still a constitutional right to an abortion, but clinics and doctors within a state are not obligated to perform the procedure.

- In 2016, the *Whole Women's Health v. Hellerstedt* ruling declared that a state cannot require abortion clinics to have admitting privileges at a local hospital in order to be licensed, calling the rule medically unnecessary and an undue burden on the right to an abortion because it would result in clinic closures. That ruling was upheld again four years later in *June v. Russo*, despite a more conservative bench due to two new Trump appointees. These newest justices made it clear that they did not respect the idea of upholding precedent— although luckily Chief Justice John Roberts did and in a 5–4 decision the new licensure rules were not put into effect.

▪ Since that decision, extreme conservative Amy Coney Barrett replaced liberal justice Ruth Bader Ginsburg, tipping the court even further to the right.

▪ A different version of this scenario may already be in play in some states where licensing requirements, onerous state laws, and other factors have combined to leave some clinics' abortion providers open in name only. One example is in Missouri, where licensing requirements combined with a seventy-two-hour waiting period and two mandatory in-person appointments made it difficult for the only clinic in the state to continue to offer abortions in 2019. After a court dispute, the Planned Parenthood of St. Louis was able to retain its license to provide abortions, but primarily refers its patients to a new Planned Parenthood affiliate clinic launched just across the river in Illinois—a mere twenty miles away and without the multi-day waiting period to prohibit immediate care.

▪ In another example, South Dakota's only abortion clinic spent much of the COVID pandemic unable to find a provider who could travel into the state to offer services. Like Missouri, the state has a seventy-two-hour waiting period with two mandatory in-person appointments, and a ban on telemedicine appointments even when a patient requests medication abortion, making it impossible for the clinic to provide care. There has not been an abortion provided in that clinic since March, and it is unclear whether services will ever resume.

- Abortion is technically legal in both South Dakota and Missouri. But in both cases patients are being urged or directly forced to go to other states to get them. That is how *Roe* gets overturned without anyone really noticing at all.

Unlikely but Still Possible

5) The court could hear an abortion case and decide that the Fourteenth Amendment guarantees a right to life to all and that outweighs the right to privacy found in *Roe*. Abortion is now illegal everywhere.

- This one seems the least likely, as it would be too much of a change too fast and would guarantee the end of the GOP as a political power. It could happen eventually, but not unless the Republican Party gets to a point where it is so embedded in its majorities that it never needs to fear reelection again.

What Does This Mean for the Clinics Left Behind?

With the clinics that do remain, being able to book an appointment will be more difficult than ever. In Texas, when clinics closed because of the passage of the Texas Omnibus Abortion Bill (HB 2), which required all abortion providers to have local hospital admitting privileges, those few remaining clinics that could still operate were telling patients of wait times of up to a month before they could come in to end a pregnancy.[7] While some of those clinics reopened after the Supreme Court ruled HB 2 was an undue burden on the right to an abortion, that period is a stark foreshadowing of what America could look like post-*Roe*.

Plus, if abortion is only available in certain states, abortion opponents will increase their presence at those clinics that do remain, hoping to close them one by one. With fewer clinics to concentrate on, the "sidewalk counseling," protests, street preaching, and monitoring for alleged medical violations will increase in frequency, especially in states bordering those where abortion is illegal.

That also means that it will be far more difficult for those patients who need care to get inside. Besides the sea of bodies that encircles some abortion clinics currently—made up of both those who oppose abortion and those who are trying to help a patient access a clinic—an increased presence of protesters can often bring additional security or police, a situation that creates a far more volatile environment for those who are undocumented, who are of communities of color, or who have other reasons to mistrust officers. Escorts have reported experiences with patients who were afraid to enter clinics, worried that the law enforcement that was outside attempting to maintain order in more aggressive protests was actually there to search or arrest patients. For some patients, the presence of security can be just as intimidating as a screaming preacher or a gory abortion photo.

We will discuss the efforts of protesters at clinics later in the book.

What Happens When Abortion Is Illegal?

Abortion opponents frequently say it is overblown to claim that making abortion illegal puts those who can become pregnant in physical danger. You can expect them to consistently bring up Ireland having one of the lowest maternal mortality rates in the world despite decades under a total abortion ban (a ban that the general population overwhelmingly voted to toss out in a national referendum in 2018).

What the anti-abortion advocates ignore is that in Ireland, people frequently obtained abortions despite the ban, either by leaving to get a termination across the border in a country with less restrictive laws, or by obtaining medication through the mail to terminate in private. It was only those who could not do so—immigrants who couldn't leave the country, the poor, those trying to hide their pregnancies from partners or family members—who were forced to carry to term.

That same trend occurs throughout the world when it comes to abortion being illegal—it does not stop people from seeking it, it only divides them into those who have the resources to find a safe abortion where it is legal, and those who attempt illegal abortions with a variety of success.

According to the Guttmacher Institute, an international reproductive rights policy nonprofit, in Latin America and the Caribbean, where abortion is highly restricted or completely illegal in nearly every country, an estimated 6.5 million abortions still occur every year, at a rate of 44 per 1,000 women. Of those abortions, only one-fourth are considered "safe" abortions—i.e., abortions conducted using World Health Organization (WHO) protocols *and* carried out by trained providers. There are on average approximately 760,000 complications from unsafe abortions per year, and in 2014 approximately 10 percent of maternal deaths in that region (900 fatalities) were caused by unsafe abortions.[8]

Lack of access to safe, legal abortion *does* and *will continue* to kill those who have unwanted pregnancies—and it will be marginalized communities lacking the financial resources to find alternative methods that will suffer the most. Removing abortion restrictions and other barriers—especially financial ones—so people can terminate in trained medical settings if they choose to is always the best option, and the one we should be fighting for. But there are also ways to make obtaining abortions outside a medical setting safer, both physically and legally, and we will discuss these later in the book.

Chapter 1 Worksheet

Would You Want to Have an Abortion?

Abortion is an extremely personal decision and one that each person needs to think through for themselves. It is also a decision that may look different at different points in your life—some people who have abortions already have children, others will go on to have children later, some will never have children at all. All options are valid and no one knows another person's circumstances. But if you think you may have an unintended pregnancy—either now or at some point in your future—here are a few questions you can ask yourself to decide if an abortion is the right choice for you. You can also visit Before and After Abortion (www.Beforeandafterabortion.com) for more assistance in addressing your decision.

1) Do I want to have a baby?
2) Can I afford to have a child?
3) Who will help me raise a child/can I raise a child by myself?
4) How will this affect my family/other children/job/education?
5) How would I feel about having an abortion? (Do I have religious, moral, ethical, or societal concerns about ending a pregnancy that might affect me?)
6) How would I feel about birth and adoption? (Would I feel unable to go through childbirth, relinquish a child, or raise a child if I changed my mind?)
7) Is my body healthy enough to be pregnant and deliver?
8) Am I mentally and emotionally able to be pregnant?
9) Am I in a relationship that would require me to hide a pregnancy from a partner or family?
10) Will I be able to access prenatal and postnatal care?

Roe Is Over—What Does That Look Like?

As the first chapter explains, it is highly unlikely that abortion is going to be made entirely illegal in the United States any time in the near future. What is likely is that a number of states are not going to have legal, accessible abortion anymore very soon—either because *Roe* is overturned and those states choose to make abortion illegal within their borders, or because *Roe* is left in place but is so decimated that those states can still close all of their clinics or place enough restrictions that an abortion is impossible to obtain (for example, if a state passes a seventy-two-hour waiting period requirement and has a six-week ban, it has made it virtually impossible to get an abortion while still technically allowing it to remain legal).

What Does Access Look Like Today, and What Could It Look Like Post-*Roe*?

In May 2018, researchers from Advancing New Standards in Reproductive Health (ANSIRH) at the University of California created a map they said showed the "abortion deserts" in the continental US. Using color coding to depict current clinic locations and populations based on how far away people lived from the nearest clinic, they showed that most of America is a spotted wasteland where pregnant people live over a hundred miles from care.

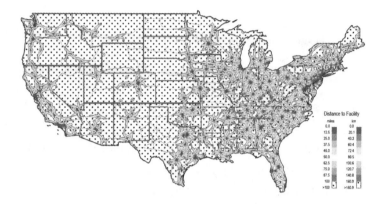

The map is alarming, but it is even more alarming if you remove those clinics that reside in states that are likely to make abortion illegal. Then you are left with this instead.

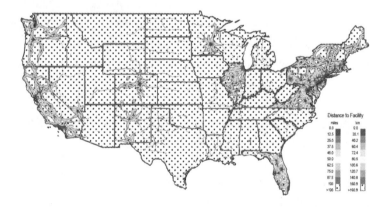

While most maps show which states likely will and won't have legal abortion, few show the real impact of how few clinics would remain in the states that may be left to provide abortions to patients. Using the direst predictions, in the Midwest access would be limited almost exclusively to Minneapolis and Chicago. In the South there would be no care between the westernmost part of Texas and the eastern half of Florida. Even worse, with the passage of a parental consent law in Florida in July 2020, the state's previously solid constitutional right to an abortion was weakened, making it possible that abortion will eventually become illegal there too.

This is likely the worst-case scenario we will be fighting when *Roe* is gone.

So what is the basis for predicting this sea of red taking over the United States? This is the most likely scenario based on a current study of existing laws, proposed laws, and the general hostility toward abortion rights from state legislatures. Information has been gathered from the Center for Reproductive Rights, the Guttmacher Institute, NARAL Pro-Choice America, Kaiser Health News, and the Safe Place Project, and was updated during the summer of 2020.

Alabama

In 2019, Alabama's legislature passed a total abortion ban that has no exceptions. That ban was blocked by a federal judge but would go into effect if *Roe* is overturned.

Alaska

Alaska does not have a trigger law and does say that there is a constitutional right to an abortion in the state constitution. At this point abortion cannot be restricted prior to viability. However, due to current restrictions in the state it is virtually impossible to get an abortion after the first trimester.

Arizona

Arizona has a ban on abortions that existed prior to *Roe* and would likely reappear if *Roe* is overturned. Arizona is unlikely to allow legal abortion in any case except if the pregnant person's life is in danger. There is no exception for sexual assault.

Arkansas

Arkansas also has a ban on abortions that existed prior to *Roe* and would likely be restored if *Roe* is overturned. The state also has "personhood" language in its constitution that allows it to promote laws that "protect the life of the unborn" from the point of conception. Arkansas's abortion ban and current language allow no exceptions of any kind when it comes to a termination.

California

Of all the states in the US, California is best prepared if *Roe* is overturned. The state protects abortion rights in its constitution and allows public insurance to pay for abortion procedures, and has approximately 150 clinics within its borders. California also allows medication abortion to be dispensed in on-campus health centers and is expanding who is allowed to provide medication abortion to patients and perform some early first-trimester non-medication abortion procedures.

Colorado

Colorado does not have any pre-*Roe* laws on the books, but it also does not enshrine the right to an abortion in its state constitution, leaving it vulnerable to legislative attacks when *Roe* is overturned. Although the state tends to elect pro–abortion rights legislators, there is always a risk of a shift in power in the state House.

Connecticut

Connecticut has no pre-*Roe* bans and does protect abortion rights in its legislation, although there is no protection in the state constitution itself.

Delaware

Delaware will continue to have abortion access post-*Roe*, having removed its pre-*Roe* ban from the law books in 2017.

Florida

The state of Florida currently declares a right to an abortion in the state constitution—but that right could be overturned in the courts due to a much more conservative bench elected in 2018. A reversal could be a devastating blow for much of the South.

Georgia

Georgia's legislature passed a so-called heartbeat ban in 2019, one that essentially bans abortion at six weeks after the last menstrual period or about two weeks after a missed cycle. The ban also makes it a felony to "assist" with an abortion, which raises the concern that a pregnant person or their companion could be arrested if they leave the state to obtain a termination. This law is currently blocked but would be able to go into effect if *Roe* is overturned.

Hawaii

Hawaii was one of the first states to make abortion legal and will likely keep all rights intact regardless of what happens to *Roe*. Recent legislation has expanded who can provide abortions and a telemedicine abortion program is currently in effect in the state.

Idaho

In 2020, Idaho's governor signed a trigger law to make abortion illegal if *Roe* is overturned.

Illinois

In 2019 the Illinois legislature passed the Reproductive Health Act, which declared abortion a fundamental right in the state and struck all lingering restrictions from the state code. Illinois, which also allows Medicaid to fund abortion procedures, is building itself into a Midwest hub for those who may lose access in nearby states.

Indiana

It's no surprise that the former home of Vice President Mike Pence will likely make abortion illegal if *Roe* is overturned. Although there isn't a trigger law, the number of abortion opponents in the state legislature (a veto-proof majority) makes creating a new ban a basic formality and one you should assume will happen.

Iowa

Iowa's state constitution says abortion is a right—but the state legislature passed a new twenty-four-hour waiting period bill in 2020 that will come before a new, more conservative state supreme court. It is unclear if the right to an abortion will survive this challenge.

Kansas

The state supreme court affirmed a right to abortion in the Kansas state constitution, but their ruling has led conservatives to push for a constitutional amendment to strip that right away. Their 2020 attempt to get the amendment on the ballot for a public vote failed, leaving abortion rights tenuous but intact for now.

Kentucky

Kentucky is very likely to ban all abortion if given the opportunity through the Supreme Court. The state is already in the process of trying to close the only clinic in operation, located in Louisville. That clinic is inundated by a mass of protesters nearly every single day it is open. It also passed a so-called heartbeat ban in 2019, making it one of nearly a dozen states that bans abortion within two weeks of a late period.

Louisiana

Louisiana still has a pre-*Roe* abortion ban on its books, and it also has a trigger law that will ban all abortion if *Roe* is overturned. In 2019 it passed a "heartbeat" ban, but that was blocked by a judge. While clinics won and were able to strike down the admitting privileges rule in 2020's *June v. Russo*, you can be sure lawmakers will be back with more restrictions and bans.

Maine

With some abortion protections already in place, abortion should remain accessible in Maine if *Roe* is overturned—as long as a slate of anti-abortion legislators isn't elected anytime soon. Maine is also piloting a program of "no touch/low touch" medication abortion services that allow more patients to obtain abortion pills without a physical exam.

Maryland

Maryland protects the right to an abortion in the state, and it currently has some of the least restrictive laws in the country. It is home to one of just three clinics in the country that provide third-trimester abortion procedures in cases of sexual assault, fetal anomalies, and other issues.

Massachusetts

Working proactively, the state just passed the NASTY Woman Act, which repealed all of Massachusetts's pre-*Roe* bans.

Michigan

Michigan has rapidly become a state with highly restricted abortion access, and it still has a pre-*Roe* ban on the books. Although there is a Democratic governor in office, abortion opponents are circumventing her and attempting to pass even more restrictions via ballot initiatives.

making it likely that the state will keep abortion legal regardless of what the Supreme Court does.

New Mexico

Despite having a pre-*Roe* ban still on the books, New Mexico has minimal abortion restrictions currently and is home to one of only three third-trimester clinics in the country. But despite the election of a new Democratic governor in 2018, the legislature has been unable to remove the pre-*Roe* restrictions from state law.

New York

New York, unsurprisingly, is safe. To tie up any loose ends, the legislature passed the Reproductive Health Act in 2019, which allows providers to offer termination in the third trimester in cases of sexual assault or fetal anomaly. The law also completely removes abortion from the penal code—a move that is expected to protect pregnant people from being investigated for suspected self-induced abortions.

North Carolina

Considering the fact that the state was once so desperate to pass abortion restrictions that it actually grafted them inside a bill about motorcycle safety in order to get it through committee,[9] it's kind of a shock to learn there is no ban on abortion if *Roe* is overturned. That may or may not last—the state was already restricting access clinic by clinic in 2013; it probably will move aggressively to cut off even more access if it has the opportunity.

North Dakota

The state of North Dakota currently has a trigger law that will make abortion illegal if *Roe* is overturned just as soon as the legislature can act.

Ohio

It took almost a decade, but Ohio finally managed to pass a so-called heartbeat ban in 2019. Like every similar ban it was blocked by the courts, but the state has aggressively sought out all means possible to block abortion access and will no doubt make it entirely illegal if Roe is overturned. In the last decade, Ohio has lost more than half of its abortion providers, leaving it with just eight clinics in the state.

Oklahoma

There is a pre-*Roe* ban on abortion still on the books in the state, and considering there are legislators who proposed a bill that explicitly states a pregnant person should be charged if caught obtaining an illegal abortion, you can bet the state will enforce that ban.

Oregon

Oregon is one of the most pro-choice states in the nation and does not have abortion restrictions. In 2019 it added free abortion for all people—including undocumented immigrants—to its insurance requirements. However, most clinics do not provide care after the first trimester and many of the clinics are located in the Portland area.

Pennsylvania

As in a number of states, what happens in Pennsylvania depends primarily on who is in the governor's office: a pro-choice governor is likely to veto new restrictions, and one who opposes abortion will probably sign them. Democrat Tom Wolf won the governor's race in 2018, making legal abortion in the state safe for now. Of course, abortion access is already limited, with most of the state's clinics located in the southeast corner.

Rhode Island

Rhode Island passed legislation codifying the right to an abortion prior to fetal viability.

South Carolina

South Carolina would be very likely to make abortion illegal, although there is no trigger law in place yet.

South Dakota

Like its neighbor to the north, South Dakota also has a trigger law for when *Roe* is overturned—but it goes into effect the very minute the Supreme Court acts. As of 2020, the COVID pandemic has made it impossible for a doctor to come to the state's only clinic to provide abortion care, leaving South Dakota one of two states in the nation where abortion is technically legal but impossible to legally obtain.

Tennessee

Tennessee held a statewide vote in 2014 that allowed residents to decide if abortion rights protections should be stripped from the state constitution—and the voters said yes. In 2019 the legislature passed a trigger ban to make abortion illegal once *Roe* is overturned.

Texas

Considering the state of Texas was the "Wade" in *Roe v. Wade*, you can be sure it will immediately revert back to a total abortion ban. It even has its original ban still lurking, waiting for a reversal from the court. Just look at how quickly the governor closed every clinic in the state during the COVID-19 pandemic in 2020—and how hard he fought to keep them closed even once non-essential medical procedures were allowed to resume—and you get a clear picture of how eager Texas is to end abortion altogether.

Utah

Wondering where Utah will fall if *Roe* goes down? Check out some of its statutory language. According to the Center for Reproductive Rights, "[S]tate policy is that 'unborn children have inherent and inalienable rights' and Utah legislature intends to 'protect and guarantee to unborn children their inherent and inalienable right to life . . .' and that woman's liberty interest to abortion only applies in cases of rape, incest, fetal anomaly, or where woman's life or health are seriously threatened."[10] That's pretty explicit—as is Utah's pre-*Roe* ban, which it kept on the books.

Vermont

Vermont repealed its pre-*Roe* ban just a few years ago, leaving it very likely to keep abortion legal regardless of what the Supreme Court does. There are currently no state restrictions in place.

Virginia

In 2020, Virginia stripped virtually all of its decades-long abortion restrictions from the books—including mandatory waiting periods and restrictions on who is allowed to provide abortion care.

Washington

Like the rest of the West Coast, Washington will be keeping abortion legal to the fullest extent it is allowed under federal law.

Washington, DC

At this point DC has no restrictions, but it is important to remember that because it is not a state, it is subject to the whims of Congress (which is why the city allows Medicaid to fund abortions whenever Democrats control congress, and and rescinds that rule whenever the GOP has control).

West Virginia

West Virginia still has a ban on abortion from before the *Roe* decision, so it is likely the state will make abortion illegal if *Roe* is reversed. Voters also narrowly passed an amendment in the 2018 midterms that states that "Nothing in this Constitution secures or protects a right to abortion or requires the funding of abortion," in preparation for a total post-*Roe* ban.

Wisconsin

The state government in Wisconsin took a hard right after the 2010 election, and as of 2018 it has yet to pivot back. The biggest threat to abortion rights has been Governor Scott Walker, who has signed every ban and restriction that came to his desk. Walker was defeated in the 2018 midterms by Democrat Tony Evers, opening up the possibility of reversing current laws, creating new protections, and eliminating the state's pre-*Roe* ban. Unfortunately, with a Republican-controlled state legislature, very little has happened.

Wyoming

Wyoming has no major abortion restrictions other than a parental consent requirement, but it also has abortion opponents holding most of the power in the state legislature and governor's office. Those two facts together make a post-*Roe* scenario hard to predict, but with only one abortion clinic in the state—in Jackson Hole—any new bills could have an immediate and devastating impact even if they don't make abortion illegal altogether.

A list of all states, their open clinics, and their gestational limits can be found in the Resource Guide in the back of the book in the "State Resources" section.

What to Know About Abortion Providers

As the previous section explains, nearly half the states in the country could be without legal abortion providers if *Roe* is overturned. But even with abortion legal in every state, abortion clinics are few and far between in much of the country. That's a concern for anyone seeking an abortion outside the West Coast or Northeast, and it's one that is exacerbated by misinformation or lack of knowledge about the clinic landscape itself.

Planned Parenthood Clinics Are NOT the Only Abortion Providers

One of the biggest misconceptions abortion seekers and abortion rights allies often have is that a person can only get an abortion at Planned Parenthood clinics. Not only is this untrue, it is a mistake that can lead many people to believe they have no options in their state at all.

According to the Abortion Care Network—an organization for independent abortion clinics across the nation—60 percent of all abortions are actually performed by non–Planned Parenthood clinics.[11] And that percentage is even higher for later-gestation abortions.

Of the seven clinics in the country that are currently the only clinic operating in their state, five are independent abortion providers. In states such as Louisiana and Alabama, where only three clinics remain, all are independent abortion clinics.

The assumption that Planned Parenthood is the only abortion provider is a dangerous one that can put the procedure out of reach for many pregnant people who may have a closer or quicker option and not know it. It also can be an enormous barrier for a person who is later in their pregnancy, since many Planned Parenthood clinics don't provide care in the later gestational weeks.

Be sure you have all the available information before booking an appointment at a clinic. If you or someone you know needs assistance, the online tool Ineedana provides clinic options based on your location and length of pregnancy.

While there are different abortion directories available, Ineedana is currently the most comprehensive listing of clinics, with results ordered by their relevance to your given situation. To use the website, enter your zip code, age, and approximately how far along you believe the pregnancy to be. None of this information is cached and it should be unidentifiable.

The resulting list will give you the closest clinics to you that provide abortion services based on your gestation. The guide will also provide additional information if you specify that you are under eighteen, such as whether you will need parental permission or who to contact for assistance getting a judicial bypass so that you can terminate without notifying a parent or guardian. This information is especially important for those who have advanced past the point where medication abortion is effective, and for those who might be in or nearing the second trimester, since many providers only offer first-trimester abortion care.

Ineedana also offers links to resources for those who may need financial assistance, lodging assistance, or other help obtaining abortion care. Because the site is independent of any abortion providers and regularly monitors for changes in clinic closings, hours of operation, and new laws, it can be relied on to always provide the most accurate information.

Ineedana can be accessed at www.ineedana.com. For privacy and potential security, it is best to open it on a private browser and clear your web cache afterward (we will talk more about Internet security and why it is so vital later in the book).

Chapter 2 Worksheet
Where Are the Clinics?

Are you or someone you know pregnant and looking for an abortion clinic? Here are the questions to ask to ensure you find the right provider.

1) *How far along in your pregnancy are you?* (Pregnancy is tracked from the point of the first day of your last menstrual period. At the point at which you miss your period you are usually considered four weeks pregnant. This is only a rough estimate, since many people have irregular periods).

2) *Would you prefer a medication or procedural abortion?* (If you are under ten weeks pregnant you can choose either. Some prefer medication so they can be in charge of their own termination and in the privacy of their home. Others choose a procedure like vacuum aspiration so it can be completed more quickly and with very little possibility of an incomplete abortion requiring a second procedure. Both options have advantages and disadvantages to consider.)

3) *Can you do a telemedicine abortion?* (Currently telemedicine abortion with medication is available in Colorado, Georgia, Hawaii, Illinois, Iowa, Maine, Maryland, Washington, DC, Minnesota, Montana, New Mexico, New York, Oregon, and Washington. This option allows you to visit a local health care provider and then consult with a doctor over video conference and have pills mailed to your home, rather than visiting an abortion clinic.)

4) *Are you later than fifteen weeks' gestation?* (Needing a second-trimester procedure may limit the clinics you can use.) Later than twenty weeks? (This may change the procedure type and require more than one day at the clinic because of the time it takes to open the cervix.) Later than twenty-four weeks? (This could be a greater challenge, as some states have laws banning abortion at particular gestational points in the pregnancy, especially at twenty-four weeks and beyond, at which point the fetus is considered to be viable—that is, able to survive outside the womb with medical assistance.)

5) *Are you in a state that requires an in-person counseling visit or ultrasound, then a mandatory waiting period before you can return for the abortion?* If so, are you within a reasonable distance of another state where this isn't required? (You may find it more efficient to travel a few hours to spend one day at a clinic, rather than having to spend multiple days receiving care at a clinic in your state. You can see which states require mandatory in-person visits at Guttmacher Institute, https://www.guttmacher.org/state-policy/explore/counseling-and-waiting-periods-abortion.)

Once you have determined the length of your pregnancy, you can enter that and your zip code into www.ineeda.com to get a list of the closest clinics that can provide care.

3

Planning for Your Own Emergencies

Yes, abortion access is soon going to be even more limited than ever—maybe even illegal. But there are steps you can take now in order to be ready for anything in a post-*Roe* landscape. This chapter is about how to prevent pregnancy, help others prevent pregnancy, start a personal abortion fund, and talk to your doctor about abortion, birth control, and other reproductive needs now so you aren't blindsided later.

So, Where Do Babies Come From?

Before we can even talk about preventing pregnancy or abortion, first we need to get some basic sex-education facts out of the way. Thanks to decades of abstinence-only sex education, not everyone knows all the basics of human reproduction besides "sperm and egg meet and that makes a baby."

To be able to prevent pregnancy, have an abortion, get pregnant, or give birth, it's important that you fully understand the basics of the menstrual cycle itself—and especially how ovulation and fertilization work.

A person who is capable of becoming pregnant has a menstrual cycle that begins functioning during puberty and will continue more or less regularly until menopause—roughly thirty to forty years. The typical menstrual cycle starts with Day 1—the first day of menstruation, or the point at which the uterus sloughs off its lining, resulting in cramping and menstrual bleeding.

A typical menstrual cycle is around twenty-eight days and repeats the same pattern: once menstruation is over, the uterine lining grows thick again, and the ovaries prepare a new egg to be released (ovulation). Ovulation in this scenario happens at around Day 14 of the cycle. If live sperm is present either when the egg is released or within twenty-four hours of ovulation, fertilization will happen, and the newly fertilized egg will begin to travel to the uterus and embed into the lining, a process that takes anywhere from seven to ten days. If it does not get fertilized, it will be passed with the rest of the uterine lining a few days later, which results in menstruation and takes the cycle back to Day 1.

For those who have longer or irregular periods, the length of time between Day 1 and ovulation—the follicular phase—can be longer or shorter, or it may vary from one cycle to the next. However, the latter half of the cycle, the luteal phase (from ovulation to menstruation), will always be the same length of time, cycle after cycle, varying from one to the next by no more than a day. Typically, the luteal phase lasts around fourteen days, much like the follicular phase, which is why the general pattern is menstruation on Day 1, ovulation on Day 14, then menstruation again after a full-twenty-eight days, cycling back to Day 1. The exception is if fertilization has occurred—then egg implantation happens somewhere around Day 21 to 24.

It is vitally important to understand the menstrual cycle in order to know not just how reproduction actually occurs, but also how anti-abortion activists manipulate terms to push their agenda. They purposely confuse gestational age and post-fertilization age, despite there being a full two weeks of difference between them (fertilization happens at about Day 14 in a cycle, but gestational age starts from Day 1, the first day of the last menstrual period). Then they write laws banning abortion at "twenty weeks," leaving pregnant people to think it is illegal at twenty weeks' gestation rather than twenty-two weeks' gestation. And even worse, the definition of "viability" used in anti-abortion legislation often varies from state to state. This is done to be deliberately confusing, as well as to give the impression that viability occurs earlier than it actually does (at this point, despite all medical advances, there is still no record of any fetus surviving birth prior to twenty-one weeks four days' gestation).

Anti-abortion activists also redefine pregnancy as occurring at the point of fertilization, rather than at the medically accepted point of implantation of the fertilized egg. Abortion opponents claim that doctors define pregnancy as beginning at implantation so that medications like birth control pills, EC, injections, implants or devices like IUDs are categorized as "contraception" (stopping a pregnancy from occurring) rather than abortion (the interruption of a pregnancy that has already begun). Anti-abortion activists refer to these methods as being "abortifacient (i.e., they stop a fertilized egg from implanting in the uterine lining), and because of that they are morally objectionable. The fact is that there is no medical way to determine if a person is pregnant until an egg implants, which is when it begins producing the hormone human chorionic gonadotropin (hCG). It is this hormone that shows up in urine and blood pregnancy tests.

Those who oppose abortion and all hormonal birth control obfuscate the medical definitions of pregnancy, gestational age, and more, and because sex education has become so politicized it is growing even harder to sort out the facts. So the important things to know are the following:

1) There are approximately five days in a cycle where a person can get pregnant—the three days prior to ovulation, the day of ovulation, and the day after ovulation. This is because sperm can live up to five days in the uterus and fallopian tubes. But unless you are specifically aware of exactly when you ovulate, this information won't help you a lot, especially if you have irregular cycles.

2) From the point at which you ovulate and the egg is fertilized to the point at which it implants (hopefully in the uterine lining but sometimes outside the uterus—this is known as an ectopic pregnancy and needs immediate medical intervention), there is no blood or urine test that can show you that an egg was fertilized.

3) When implantation occurs, hCG production begins and doubles every forty-eight to seventy-two hours. Once the level is above 5 mIU/ml, it can be detected by blood test and is the threshold for being medically "pregnant." Many home pregnancy urine tests can show positive results at 10 mIU/ml. In a number of cases this could happen before a person has even missed their period.

4) Most forms of hormonal contraception work by stopping ovulation and/or making the mucus in the cervix hostile to sperm—two ways to prevent fertilization. Emergency contraception works by delaying ovulation after unprotected sex so that sperm already in the uterus and fallopian tubes will die prior to an egg being released. None of these things are "abortions," even if you do believe that pregnancy begins at fertilization rather than at the medically accepted point of implantation.

Emergency Contraception (EC)

If your first thought when Supreme Court Justice Anthony Kennedy announced his retirement, or when Ruth Bader Ginsburg passed away, was "Abortion is going to be illegal! I'm going to make a Plan B stockpile!," well, you aren't alone. Just like after Donald Trump's Electoral College victory, social media exploded with tweets and posts about people purchasing Plan B to have on hand either for themselves, family and friends, or even strangers lacking access to a clinic.

Having a dose or two of emergency contraception available is always a good idea, regardless of the legality of abortion or birth control options. EC works prior to ovulation, preventing an egg from being released at a time when sperm may be present and stopping fertilization. Although some forms of EC can work for as long as a week after unprotected sex, most are at their most effective when taken within seventy-two hours of intercourse. Having a supply on hand allows more people to effectively take the medication at its optimal time to prevent pregnancy, and it eliminates issues like getting into a doctor or clinic for ella (ulipristal acetate, which is more effective than Plan B but also requires a prescription), finding a pharmacy that carries it, getting into a clinic that will offer it, or, in cases of sexual assault, going immediately to an emergency room for dosage, especially if that hospital ends up being religiously affiliated and refuses to provide the medication.

And, as we saw during the COVID-19 pandemic, sometimes none of these options are even available. No one wants to risk exposure to a virus just to be able to obtain EC if they don't need to. Having one or maybe two doses on hand, before they are needed, just makes common sense.

However, there is a vast difference between having a dose (or doses) for an emergency and "stockpiling" them for personal use or distribution. Here are some things to consider to ensure you are acquiring EC in the best way possible.

1) Are you buying locally, or online?
    ▪ If you are purchasing emergency contraception for future use, please consider only buying it from online sites. This ensures that for those who have an actual emergency and need medication immediately, there is still a supply on the shelf for them to buy and it isn't out of stock. Waiting two days or more for delivery because there is no place to purchase locally is the surest way for a person to end up with an unwanted pregnancy.
2) Do you really need that many doses?
    ▪ Yes, buying a bunch of EC feels like a really proactive way to stick it to Trump and the rest of the anti-abortion politicians. But remember, most EC has a shelf life of three to four years, and in some cases the clock may already be ticking. Twenty packs of EC do no one any good if they all expire because you really only needed four. Unless you have a real reason to think that you might end up as a distribution channel for your friends or neighbors, limit how many you get at once. Odds are, you will be able to buy more later.
3) Is there a local organization that offers EC? Can you help them, instead?
    ▪ Let's be frank, getting emergency contraception from a stranger is a sort of freaky idea. Preventing a pregnancy— especially after intercourse—is a pretty private activity. No one really wants to reach out to someone they don't know in order to get medication, but they are more likely to con-

tact reproductive rights and justice groups, organizations that support marginalized communities, or feminist groups than private individuals. Don't recreate the wheel when there are already organizations distributing EC—offer those groups money or medication, or even offer to help distribute through their channels rather than try to do this alone.

EC access has changed a lot in just the last few years, and thanks to a lot of organizations providing funding, it's easier than ever to access for free or at low cost.

Purchase Your Own

For people looking for medication that will be delivered straight to their home, Afterpill.com is a website where you can purchase single-dose or three-dose packages of EC for twenty dollars each—less than half of what you'd pay at a pharmacy.

Or if you are already getting birth control pills by mail, either through a Planned Parenthood clinic or via an online pharmacy, ask about having a dose or two of EC added to your next delivery. Some outlets—especially Planned Parenthoods—will offer one or two doses a year that they will send along as part of your prescription. Or you can ask your doctor to write a prescription for ella to fill now and have on hand for later, when you or someone you know might need it.

Get It On Campus

A new pilot program has begun providing EC on college campuses via vending machines. This option allows students to be able to obtain medication without needing to visit a health center or a dorm adviser, ensuring more privacy as well as 24-7 accessibility.

So far only thirteen colleges across the United States have EC available in vending machines on campus, but the American Society for Emergency Contraception is working to expand that number. If you would like to try to bring a machine to your local campus, contact asec@americansocietyforec.org.

Get Free EC by Mail

The Yellowhammer Fund, an abortion fund and reproductive justice organization in Alabama (disclosure: I currently work for the fund as its communications director), offers free EC by mail to anyone in Alabama, Mississippi, or the Florida Panhandle, with hopes of spreading the program further in the South as supplies allow. You can see if you qualify and order your own EC at www.yellowhammerfund.org.

Here is a list of other places that currently provide emergency contraception distribution that you can contact and support:

Alabama Reproductive Rights Advocates (ARRA) (Alabama)
2824 Hunterwood Dr. SE, Decatur, AL 35603
865-465-9793
http://alabamareproductiverightsadvocates.com
lindadfoundation@gmail.com

Plan B NOLA (New Orleans Area)
504-264-3656
https://www.planbnola.com/

IndyFeminists (Indiana)
https://www.facebook.com/IndyFems/
(At this point IndyFeminists only communicates via Facebook Messenger.)

Mississippi Reproductive Freedom Fund (Mississippi)
2210 Hill Ave., Jackson, MS 39211
769-218-9413
https://msreprofreedomfund.org/
mississippireprofreedomfund@gmail.com

Kentucky Health Justice Network
PO Box 4761, Louisville, KY 40204
1-855-576-4576
https://kentuckyhealthjusticenetwork.org/
info@khjn.com

What You Need to Know About Emergency Contraception

First of all, just a friendly reminder that when we talk about EC, we tend to go straight to a discussion about medication. But when it comes to dealing with the aftermath of unprotected sex, the copper IUD is the most effective form of EC and can be placed by a practitioner up to five days after unprotected intercourse. Keep that in mind if you were already considering long-lasting contraception options—but obviously don't jump into an IUD just as a means of preventing a possible pregnancy after unprotected sex.

Of course, you can't keep an IUD lying around in case of emergencies like you can with pills. When it comes to medication EC, there are multiple brands, all with different price points and best practices. Plan B One Step, Next Choice One Dose, Take Action, My Way, and AfterPill all work up to five days post–unprotected sex but are most successful when taken within the first seventy-two hours. All are available without a prescription.[12]

Ella is more effective than Plan B when used within three days of unprotected sex, and it is also more effective for people with a higher body mass index (BMI), generally people weighing over 165 pounds. However, it can only be obtained with a prescription, and if you are already on hormonal birth control it is less effective and makes your hormonal birth control less effective, too (so you might want to consider a different medication or even a copper IUD if you are worried about getting pregnant after forgetting to take your regular birth control pill).

Who Should Really Stockpile and Distribute EC

Of course, there are some cases where it does make sense to buy a lot of EC and act as a distributor. If you are in a community with no EC provider already—especially an area without much pharmacy access—and you are willing to be a public face for distribution (and especially if you have the ability to commit to it from both a financial and time perspective), this can be a good opportunity to provide concrete help. This may also be a valuable resource if you are on a college campus (especially at a religious college, which may not offer EC at the health center, and where students may not have transit options to get to a pharmacy). Resident advisors (RAs), floor leaders, or members of reproductive rights, human rights, civil rights, or LGBTQ rights campus groups would also be excellent public faces for EC distribution in your college or university.

To prepare and lay the groundwork for your new group, go to the "Finding Your Personal Cause" and "Avoiding Surveillance" chapters and follow the tips for creating your own support network.

What to Do Instead to Ensure More Access to EC

Distributing EC is helpful, but the biggest way an individual can help those who need emergency contraception is to be sure that stores are stocking it regularly and are allowing people to purchase the medication without restrictions. EC is available for purchase regardless of gender or age and without ID. Check with all of your local retailers to ensure it is in stock, and, if not, ask them to carry it. Urge those retailers to keep it in the aisles and accessible, not behind the counter or inside a locked display. Contact the corporate offices of those stores that do have it available and thank them for keeping it on the shelves. Make sure to report any issues with purchasing (such as a pharmacist saying they have a religious objection and not finding another person to complete the transaction, a demand for ID, a refusal to sell to someone presenting as male) to the National Women's Law Center at 866-745-5487 or coverher@nwlc.org. Also contact your state pharmacy board, the corporate office of the pharmacy, and local media outlets.

Birth Control Pills

Even with abortion banned in some states, it's unlikely that birth control will be banned, too. However, it very well may get harder to access from a logistical or financial standpoint, especially if the government continues to defund family planning clinics and reallocates those funds to entities that don't offer hormonal birth control.

According to the Guttmacher Institute, the rate of unintended pregnancy among the poor is five times the rate of unintended pregnancy among those of higher income levels, and the rate among the Black community is more than double that of the white community.[13] One of the biggest barriers to pregnancy prevention is the ability to access birth control, either because of cost, no access to doctors for a prescription, or transportation issues that make obtaining pills at a pharmacy too difficult.

As of June 2018, Washington, DC, and fifteen states allow those who use the birth control pill to obtain a full year's supply at once (although some of them require you obtain a shorter supply of just a few months first, then they allow twelve months' worth). Those states are California, Colorado, Connecticut, Hawaii, Illinois, Maine, Maryland, Massachusetts, Nevada, New Jersey, New York, Oregon, Vermont, Virginia, and Washington.[14] Other states have legislation still pending. These increased birth control supplies may be able to cut down on the logistical barriers that prevent reliable birth control pill usage, especially if family planning clinics continue to close.

If you are in a twelve-month state, take advantage of the access if possible. If your state claims to offer this service but no doctors seem able to put it into practice, contact the local legislators initiating the legislation and let them know. If you are in a pending state, or your state has not brought up a bill, reach out to your legislators to see what can be done to speed the process up. Remind politicians—especially Republican ones—that if abortion is being restricted it is imperative that they do all they can to support preventing unwanted pregnancies in the first place.

You can also reach out to new online distribution channels for birth control pills—many of which will be covered by your insurance. Sites like Nurx and ThePillClub offer multiple months of a variety of contraceptive pills that can still be billed to your insurance if you have it. For more on finding birth control online, visit FreethePill.org, and click on "Who Prescribes the Pill Online?"

Can You Use Birth Control Pills as EC?

Before emergency contraception was so readily available, health clinics would sometimes give out birth control pills with special instructions on how to take them in order for them to work as emergency contraception.

Using birth control packs this way isn't nearly as necessary anymore, but it could still work in a pinch if you happen to have some around. This information on how to create an EC dose was found at the blog *A Womb of One's Own* (https://wombofonesown.wordpress.com).[15]

Not every birth control pill contains the active ingredient in Plan B. If your birth control pill does, you'll see that after the brand name, in parentheses, the word "levonorgestrel" will appear. Contraceptive pills combine levonorgestrel with other hormonal ingredients, and the dose of each ingredient will be listed on your medication packaging.

In order to use a levonorgestrel birth control pill as emergency contraception, you'll want to first compute how many pills you will need to take. First, look at how many milligrams of levonorgestrel are in each pill. For most birth control pill formulations containing levonorgestrel, this will be .5–.6 mg. This means that in order to bring the total amount of levonorgestrel to 1.5 mg, you will typically need three pills, taken in a single dose as soon as possible after having unprotected sex. 1.5 divided by the number of milligrams per pill (or 1,500 divided by the number of micrograms per pill) will give you the number of pills required.

Round UP, not down: slightly too much medication is better than slightly too little. However, it is unnecessary to use extra pills significantly beyond the 1.5 mg dosage. Many websites containing information on how to use levonorgestrel-containing birth control as emergency contraception say that women should take, depending on the brand of birth control being used, up to twelve total tablets containing .5 mg of levonorgestrel each (divided into two doses). This is unnecessary and may even be harmful. The amount of total levonorgestrel in such a dosage is substantially more likely to cause side effects—mostly of the gastrointestinal variety—without significantly enhancing the ability of the pills to prevent unwanted pregnancy.

It is absolutely essential to make sure you *only use active pills* when using contraceptive pills as Plan B. Most forms of contraceptive pills come in monthly packs that include twenty-one days of active pills and seven days of placeholder sugar pills. The three weeks of active pills are generally colored differently from the week of inactive (sugar) pills in the pill packet. Inactive pills have no medication at all, so using them won't help you to prevent a pregnancy.

Users of emergency contraception should know that EC involves the risks of taking any hormonal birth control pill (though the fact that it is taken infrequently and only for a day at a time makes long-term side effects unlikely). Many users report minor gastrointestinal distress or being nauseated. Much less frequently, blood clots have been known to form as a result of the active ingredient in these pills. Blood clots are a serious side effect (possibly even lethal if one dislodges and causes a pulmonary embolism, stroke, or heart attack) but are rare. If you notice severe leg pain, shortness of breath, or any symptoms of a stroke or heart attack after taking emergency contraception, go to the emergency room immediately—these could indicate the formation of a blood clot.

Condoms

Whether or not abortion or even birth control is legal, it's always good to have condoms on hand for pregnancy prevention and avoiding sexually transmitted infections. Buying them in bulk is cheapest, and they last four to five years. Buying condoms online is the best way to get the cheapest rate, and stick to known brands (Trojan, Durex, etc.) to ensure high quality.

Also be aware, however, that in some jurisdictions, having multiple condoms on your person can be considered "evidence" of potential sex crimes. While most states—most notably New York and California—have banned police from considering condoms as an "instrument of a crime" when arresting sex workers, prosecutors in Allegheny County, Pennsylvania, still use that as an arresting charge. Critics worry that the continued practice is leading to less-safe sex acts and the spread of STIs. Be sure to pay attention to any local laws, but also continue to practice the safest sex possible if you want to avoid pregnancy or disease.

Long-Acting Reversible Contraception (LARC)

When it comes to preventing unwanted pregnancy, there is almost nothing more effective than LARC. Implants and intrauterine devices (IUDs) have no potential for user error like birth control pills or condoms, making them the most reliable way of preventing pregnancy that's out there.

They are also far more expensive than any other method—at least out of pocket. If your insurance covers them currently, do consider taking advantage of this, as once they have been inserted they can prevent pregnancy anywhere from three (implant) to ten (copper IUD) years.

But also be aware of potential concerns before jumping into a LARC. Implants and IUDs are often difficult if not impossible to have safely removed without a health care provider's assistance. While it may not be difficult to find a doctor or clinic willing to provide one now, there could be a far larger barrier when it comes to a removal—especially an early one. This can be especially true for people of color, who have historically been subject to racial bias in the medical community and stripped of their reproductive autonomy, coerced and outright forced into birthing, birth control, and sterilization procedures without consent. A "reversible" contraceptive method is only as reliable as your access to a medical professional willing to participate. If you switch doctors over the years, or if your family planning center closes, it may be much harder to get off birth control than it was to get on it.

Another issue to weigh with LARC is which type to choose and the possible complications that might arise. Implants release etonogestrel, a form of progesterone, whereas IUDs like Mirena, Skyla, Kyleena, and Liletta release levonorgestrel, another progesterone. As with all hormonal contraceptives, you may experience some side effects like irregular spotting. Copper IUDs (ParaGard) do not have a hormonal aspect, but some people do get heavier, more painful periods. Be prepared to adjust if it turns out the LARC you begin with isn't the one that is right for you.[16]

For more information on which type of birth control might be your best fit, try the "Method Explorer" and other guides at Bedsider (www.bedsider.org).

Sterilization

Obviously if you want to completely avoid pregnancy for good in a post-*Roe* era you could seek out permanent birth control (sterilization). This procedure can be obtained by either gender, and in some states or through some insurers the costs will be covered. However, it is not meant to be reversible and will render a person permanently infertile. Be positive that this is a decision you are completely certain about before contacting a doctor.

Also, be cognizant of the historical legacy of sterilization, which has long been used by the government as a means of permanently limiting the reproductive rights of populations like poor people of color, the mentally and physically disabled, and others, either through financial coercion or without proper informed consent.

Finding a Family Planning Provider

With the protections of Obamacare disappearing, massive job loss due to the COVID-19 pandemic, the Trump administration's war against Planned Parenthood, and the Supreme Court ruling that any employer can block contraceptive coverage from their employees' insurance plans, basic preventative reproductive health care has become alarmingly difficult for many people in the United States to access. As of June 2020, there are still fourteen states in the country that have not expanded Medicaid, and with unemployment numbers reaching forty million at the same time, health insurance through employers is out of reach for many people too.

Title X funding was created to ensure that birth control and other sexual health care services were available to all populations, regardless of their ability to pay. Established in 1970 by Republican president Richard Nixon, this half-century-long program has been decimated by the Trump administration, which implemented new rules to ban any clinic affiliated with an abortion provider from receiving funding, as well as any clinic or provider that so much as *mentions* an abortion provider.

In addition, the Trump administration opened funding opportunities to faith-based medical organizations that do not offer any form of hormonal contraception at all. In 2019, the Trump administration provided $1.7 million in funding to Obria,[17] a chain of clinics in California whose birth control options consist solely of fertility tracking apps that encourage users to monitor their menstrual cycles and avoid sex during potentially fertile times—a form of contraception that has been proven to be at best 75 to 80 percent successful at preventing pregnancy.[18]

The religious Right is only getting started seeding these anti-contraception, anti–sex ed, pro-marriage "Women's Health Centers" across the country, and now that Title X funding has been opened to them, more will be coming soon. Because new Title X rules allow funding for providers even if they don't offer a "full" range of contraceptive options—and allow medical entities to object to certain services like hormonal birth control as a matter of "conscience"— this reallocation of funds will only increase. That's a terrifying thought as more and more people lose access to even basic health insurance.

So how do you find birth control and sexual health care without ending up somewhere that doesn't offer hormonal contraception, especially if you don't have insurance? Planned Parenthood is still a good resource despite the fact that the Health and Human Services Department is defunding them at a federal level. Many states still provide local funding, allowing Planned Parenthood clinics, qualified health care centers, and other reproductive health centers to offer sliding-scale contraceptive services and in-person exams. You can also look at your local health department, which should have a list of options for uninsured patients. There is also a list of Federally Qualified Health Centers (FQHCs) that you can search by zip code at https://findahealthcenter.hrsa.gov. Be aware, though, that you could end up at a religiously affiliated clinic or with a doctor who has moral objections to hormonal contraception, especially for unmarried people.

Crisis Pregnancy Centers

Anti-abortion activists call them "Women's Health Centers" or "Pregnancy Resource Centers." Pro-choice groups call them "Fake Health Clinics." Whatever you call them, Crisis Pregnancy Centers (CPCs) are a growing problem for people seeking comprehensive sexual health care and abortion options. Due to seemingly endless funding by churches and exponentially more deceptive branding practices, CPCs aren't just exploding in volume across the nation, they are confusing even the savviest people with their online ads, search engine optimization, and carefully crafted websites designed to look as if they are full-scale, full-service reproductive health clinics.

When a person is seeking an abortion, visiting a CPC when they think they are at an abortion provider can prove to be both emotionally and physically harmful. A CPC will not provide accurate information about abortion, instead presenting it as a dangerous procedure and exaggerating or outright fabricating the potential complications and risks. But an even bigger issue is that unknowingly visiting a CPC can delay the act of getting an abortion when you want one. At best, a visit to a CPC will delay an appointment at a real abortion provider, which can be especially difficult for people who don't have many nearby clinics as options and may have to wait days or longer for an appointment. Even worse, some CPCs have been known to purposely give out inaccurate dating in their ultrasounds, leading a person to believe they are either further along or less advanced in the pregnancy than they really are.

Inaccurate dating can harm a pregnant person who wants an abortion regardless of how those dates have been manipulated. Some CPC staff will tell a patient they are only a few weeks pregnant and that they have ample time to decide if they want an abortion, when in fact they may already be close to the legal limit for an abortion in the state. Others have been known to do the opposite, telling a patient they are already too late so they will not follow up with a clinic at all. Both of these are coercive practices that take away a person's right to choose.

But CPCs aren't just a concern for people who are pregnant or think they might be—they are a problem for those seeking contraceptive options too. Not only do they not provide contraception or refer for contraception, but they also counsel against using birth control altogether. They wrongly refer to IUDs as preventing implantation despite the fact that they actually prevent fertilization, and often claim that emergency contraception is a form of abortion, even though EC prevents ovulation from occurring.

In a 2018 study published in the medical journal *Contraception*, researchers studied sixty-four Georgia-based crisis pregnancy center websites, and discovered that "of the 64 websites reviewed, 20 (31%) presented information about contraceptives. Most of the content was dedicated to emergency contraception. Emphasis on risks and side effects was the most prominent theme. However, no site presented information about the frequency or prevalence of risks and side effects. Sites also emphasized contraceptive failure and minimized effectiveness. We found a high degree of inaccurate and misleading information about contraceptives."[19]

It isn't just websites that are inaccurate, either. In 2013, NARAL Pro-Choice Virginia did an undercover investigation of the state's CPCs, recording phone calls and in-person visits with the staff. These CPC workers told potential patients blatantly untrue "facts" about contraception, including claims that condoms are too porous to prevent disease, that fertility awareness–based cyclical family planning was better at preventing pregnancy than birth control pills, and even that IUDs could embed in a person's uterus, or that their strings act as a path for infections to enter the vagina.[20]

Want to know if the clinic you are considering is a CPC? You can see a full, open-sourced, updated, and verified list at https://reproaction.org/fakeclinicdatabase. And if you want to take action directly to ensure more people aren't deceived by these "clinics," opportunities to do so will be discussed later on in the book.

Having "The Talk" with Your Doctor

If you are vetting a new provider because of insurance changes, lack of insurance coverage, or another reason, or you have a regular physician whose views on bodily autonomy you haven't probed, now is the best time to have a frank discussion about where they stand on medical issues surrounding reproductive autonomy. Questions you should be asking include the following:

- Do you treat LGBTQ patients? Do you feel uncomfortable treating survivors of sexual assault?
- Do you support all forms of birth control—and will you pro-

vide nonjudgmental prenatal care—regardless of the age, gender, race, marital status, or number of children of the person asking for it?

▪ Would you support me and help facilitate things if I decided that I wanted to be sterilized, either now or down the road? (Some physicians have concerns about permanent birth control for those who are young, who have never had children, or who have never been married. While those may all be valid concerns, ultimately your physician should recognize that you should have the final say about your body.)

▪ If I became pregnant and there was a medical concern that could require an abortion, would you object to the abortion? Would you have the knowledge to perform a procedure or know who to connect me to who could perform it in the safest way possible inside a medical setting? (Especially find out if your doctor can perform or can refer you to someone who can perform a D&E in a medical emergency, rather than simply inducing labor.)

▪ Would you provide me with information if I became pregnant and did not want to give birth? Would you be willing to offer medication to end the pregnancy if it was still early, or refer me to someone who would? Would it change how you treated me, medically? Would you even still want me as a patient?

▪ Would you report illegal activities that affect my medical care to the police if I told you about them?

All of these questions can be awkward and uncomfortable, but they are also questions you need to ask now in order to determine if your doctor will always consider your physical and mental needs first. You are the patient, and their duty should always be to support your best medical outcomes.

Setting Up a Personal Emergency Abortion Fund

No one ever plans to need an abortion, but maybe everyone should, just in case. Not having the money to pay for an abortion—and the expenses surrounding it, such as time off work, travel, lodging, childcare, and more—is what causes many people to delay the procedure, which, ironically, can then drive up the costs. A look at one Las Vegas area abortion clinic's weekly price sheet shows how dramatic the increase can be. At that clinic, an abortion at fourteen weeks' gestation can be obtained for $550 or less (a price that is actually quite low compared to what many clinics in the country charge). From that point onward, it increases $100 per week for each week between weeks fourteen and seventeen, $300 a week from weeks eighteen to twenty-one, then $200 each week until twenty-three weeks' gestation, by which time the price is $2,500.[21]

For some lower-income patients it becomes a cycle they cannot break, eventually becoming too expensive for them to terminate before the gestational limit is reached. According to Advancing New Standards in Reproductive Health (ANSIRH), a research group at the University of California, San Francisco, those who cannot access services because of cost are four times as likely to be in poverty four years later than low-income people who were able to obtain their abortions.[22]

Abortion funds and practical support groups can help with all that, but as need grows and expenses increase—especially as clinics close and states cut off all legal access, forcing patients to travel farther to the fewer available clinics—these groups will only be able to do so much. If you are privileged enough to have the ability, it wouldn't hurt to save up for your own potential emergency. If you don't need it, that money can always be used somewhere else, or even eventually given to an abortion fund to assist others in need.

In the first step for setting up a personal abortion fund, consider actually investing in pregnancy tests themselves. After all, ruling a pregnancy in or out is imperative before deciding what you need to do. Consider purchasing some cheap pregnancy tests to have around so they are available if you think you might be pregnant. This is especially helpful if you happen to have irregular periods and aren't as sure of when your next cycle may be coming.

Pregnancy tests at the Dollar Store or another discount retailer are just as effective as the twenty-dollar tests you can purchase at your pharmacy, so pick up a few to have on hand. You can also purchase cheap bulk testing strips at online retailers like Amazon by searching for Wondfo, where you can get them for as little as twenty cents a strip.

But what if you do find that second line on your test? How much should you set aside to be prepared? In the wake of the Texas clinic closures following the implementation of HB 2 in 2016, *Cosmopolitan* magazine's Hannah Smothers asked Natalie St. Claire of Fund Texas Choice that very question. St. Claire's advice? Set aside enough for the procedure ($300–$1,000 for a first-trimester abortion, depending on gestational age, procedure type, anesthesia, and additional medical needs like being Rh positive), add in whatever travel you may need (gas, plane tickets, lodging, etc.), food costs for a few days, child care costs if you have young children, and two or three days' lost wages in case you need to go to a state with a waiting period or you need some recovery time and you are unable to take paid time off.[23]

Bundled together, yes, that's a lot of money. Start small as you develop your fund, working with what you know can't be covered elsewhere. First check to see if your state or private insurance covers abortion, whether you have a clinic in your state currently, and if your state is one of the ones that will ban abortion post-*Roe*, and if so where the best available clinic might be. The sooner you can terminate the pregnancy, the less it will cost, so consider things like irregular periods that make it difficult to date a pregnancy, face-to-face meetings with one or more days in between at your local provider, or how booked the clinic might be (clinics in low-access states like Montana, Mississippi, Alabama, and Louisiana often have longer waits for scheduling than in states with easy access and multiple clinics). Also think through potential decisions like waiting for vacation time to accumulate or scheduling work so you can take time off without losing a paycheck, and remember that delaying an abortion until later in gestation is likely to increase the cost.

The scenarios can be overwhelming, which is why it is good to plan ahead before this becomes an emergency.

Need a step-by-step breakdown? Here's a good "average" budget that takes into account a number of variables:

- Procedure: $700
- Gas: $50
- Airline ticket: $250
- Hotel for two nights (forty-eight-hour waiting period): $100 a night/$200
- Food: $30 a day/$90
- Childcare: $100 a day/$300

- Lost wages: $15 an hour (eight-hour days)/$360

Total fund = $750 to approximately $2,000, depending on your location and personal situation

The bill is a big one, which is why people struggle so much to pay for an abortion when the need arises. Try to set aside a little now if you can. Open a separate account just for this and set an automatic transfer for ten dollars a month, or some other small amount you aren't likely to notice. If you get a bonus or some money as a gift, toss it in there too. Even tax refunds or stimulus checks can help. None of it may seem like much, but every bit helps if you do find yourself in a real emergency.

Of course, there are groups that will help with all of this (funding, travel, meals, lodging) if you do get in a bind. Practical support groups and abortion funds are all listed in the "Finding Your Personal Cause" chapter and are also broken down by state at www.postroehandbook.com. If you need help, you will not be alone.

Chapter 3 Worksheet
How Can I Get Support for an Abortion?

Are you looking for an abortion and not sure how to pay for it? Here are some steps to take to get assistance.

1) *Find your clinic.* Use the information in the chapter 2 worksheet to identify the clinic that is your best option for terminating a pregnancy at this time.

   *My clinic is*_____

2) *Contact the clinic first.* Contacting the clinic to book an appointment should be done before anything else, in order to confirm that you are able to get in, that they have the service you want, and what the overall cost of the procedure would be. This is especially important as clinics can sometimes be closed due to staffing issues, pending legal cases, or, as we saw in the spring of 2020, restrictions from the COVID-19 health crisis.

My clinic appointment is _____

3) *Ask the clinic for financial help.* Some clinics provide direct financial support for those who cannot afford an abortion. Others will direct you to an abortion fund that works with their clinic, and either provide you with the information you need to reach out to that fund, or contact the fund on your behalf. Be aware that no fund will make a pledge unless you already have booked an appointment.

My procedure will cost _____

I have _____.

I need _____ *in funding.*

4) *Determine whether you will have non-procedural costs or logistical issues.* Are you unable to access a car when you would need to make an appointment? Will you need to stay overnight because of a waiting period, or because the clinic is too far from home and you need to be there early? Do you need a bus or plane ticket to get there? Do you have enough

money left over to eat while you are traveling? These are all additional expenses that you should contemplate while obtaining funding and ask about when you speak to the clinic or the fund the clinic connects you to. These additional items may be issues that practical support networks can assist you with, especially if you are traveling across state lines in order to access an abortion. Have a list of needs prepared before speaking with the clinic or fund.

My additional needs are _____

5) *Be prepared to advocate. A lot.* It can take a long time to get through on some of the assistance lines. You may need to call frequently, or leave a number of messages, or do a lot of follow-up. Sometimes funds will run out of money at certain points in the month, or week, or even day, depending on how their funding is allocated and what their budget is. You may find yourself needing to call one fund multiple times or multiple funds in an area in order to get the amount you need covered. Be persistent, be flexible, and most of all be patient.

My next step is to call _____ *for funding for the procedure.*

I should call _____ *for assistance with gas/hotel/food.*

Finished Checklist

My procedure is at _____

on _____

*and costs $*_____

$ _____ *is being pledged by* _____

I will be paying $ _____ *myself.*

_____ *will provide practical support.*

makes it impossible to operate a clinic it doesn't matter if the procedure is legal or not.

City councils have already become abortion clinic gatekeepers by changing zoning requirements for existing clinics or conversely by changing zoning laws to allow in those who want the clinic to shut down.

Some examples of how this works are:

1) In 2013 the city council of Fairfax City, Virginia, voted to change their zoning laws, creating a new category called "medical care facility," which would require the current abortion clinic to obtain a $4,800 special use permit as well as approval by the council itself to continue operating. As a result of the new ordinance NOVA Women's Healthcare shut down. In 2015 another city council, this time in Manassas, Virginia, followed suit, resulting in the closure of Amethyst Health Center for Women. In both cases no new clinics opened in either city because the process was too burdensome.[24]

2) In 2014, when Dalton Johnson attempted to move his abortion clinic into a new building in order to meet the new standards for clinics passed by the state of Alabama, the city council refused to offer him a zoning variance for a medical business, despite the fact that his building had previously housed a doctor's office and was also home to a dentist. While the medical variances had previously been rubber-stamped, the council forced Johnson to wait for months for approval before finally agreeing. During that period of time, there was no abortion access at all in northern Alabama.[25]

3) In October 2017 Whole Women's Health announced plans to open a new clinic in South Bend, Indiana, that would offer only medication abortions.[26] They applied for a license from the

state only to be rejected, beginning a long court process that as of July 2020 is not completely resolved. The clinic was finally granted a provisional license in the summer of 2019, nearly two years after applying, while both sides continued to fight in court. Meanwhile, a crisis pregnancy center (an anti-abortion and often religious nonprofit whose goal is to convince pregnant people not to end their pregnancies) was able to purchase a building next door to the proposed clinic and seek out a rezoning action from the city council. The rezoning process took less than two months to get official approval. Luckily, a veto of the rezoning decision by South Bend's mayor forced the crisis pregnancy center to discard their new location next door and move in across the street instead.[27]

City Councils as Funding Sources

One of the biggest effects that city councils have recently had in protecting abortion rights is a recent push to use the budget process to help people access abortion care.

In New York City in 2019, the city council approved a $250,000 grant to the New York Abortion Access Fund (NYAAF), as a means of supplementing the fund's work with low-income people seeking abortion care. While the state of New York already offers Medicaid coverage for abortion services, the NYAAF funding was offered to help those who may not be eligible for Medicaid, those who are uninsured, or those whose insurance doesn't cover abortion—especially people who come to New York for abortions because they are unable to access clinics in their own states.

A progressive city like New York providing this much additional funding for abortion access is groundbreaking. But in a red state like Texas, the work is even harder. That's why abortion rights advocates in Texas started working on a plan to gain ground inch by inch when working with the city of Austin to implement more support for those who need abortions.

NARAL Pro-Choice Texas and Lilith Fund for Reproductive Equity worked together on a multi-year approach to local funding possibilities. The first step, according to Aimee Arrambide, executive director of NARAL Pro-Choice Texas, was to assess what the city council felt comfortable doing, and working within their parameters.

In 2017, the city council agreed to introduce an "Abortion is Healthcare" declaration in an attempt to remove the stigma often associated with abortion in Texas and to re-frame the public perception around care. In contrast, a similar resolution at the county level was unsuccessful until the word "abortion" was removed and replaced with something less "controversial"—just one example of how ingrained abortion stigma can be.

The following year, the Austin City Council passed a proclamation to support "Rosie's Law," a bill meant to allow Medicaid funding for abortion in Texas. The bill was named after Rosie Jimenez, a low-income Latinx woman in the Rio Grande Valley who died after attempting an illegal abortion because she couldn't afford a legal procedure.

Then, in 2019, the council took its biggest step yet, approving $150,000 in "practical support" funding to assist those who need gas, hotels, or other support to get an abortion in Austin. Because the state of Texas forbids any state money going to abortion clinics, this practical support pool of funds helps cover the incidentals around obtaining an abortion, freeing up other money for the procedure.

Even within hostile, anti–abortion rights red states, clinics tend to exist in the more progressive cities. By going hyper-local, activists can make the biggest changes and the most direct impact, as long as they work within politicians' comfort zone.

What Else You Can Do—Direct Action

You don't need to be on the city council to help your local clinic. Here's what you can do to directly impact your city's clinic(s).

1) Go to city council meetings.
   - Check their agendas and see if they are doing anything involving zoning around your clinic.
   - Ask the council about noise ordinance enforcements or if there are any buffer zones that could be put in place to protect patients. (Contrary to popular belief, buffer zones are still legal even after the *McCullen v. Coakley* Supreme Court ruling of 2014, just not thirty-five-foot buffers.)
2) Frequent businesses that are near clinics.
   - Among the biggest problems facing clinics are landlords who do not want to continue renting to them or neighbors who are hostile to them because they believe the chaos drives away customers. When businesses aren't being harmed by— or are even benefitting from—being next to a clinic, they are far more likely to work with the clinic and support them when they are attacked by protesters or city government.
3) Support and utilize services that do business with clinics.
   - One of the ways abortion opponents try to close clinics is by intimidating their vendors. They will target the person who delivers their packages; they will harass those who repair their roof. They will call out the restaurant that drops off their lunches in the hope of completely isolating the clinic and its staff. Local clinics often ask for community support when that happens. Be there for them.
4) Offer emotional support.
   - Clinics like cards, flowers, anything that makes them feel like

they are appreciated, especially when they are being inundated with harassment. These signs of support help prevent staff burnout, and that keeps clinics open, too.

Use Your Tools to Ensure Diversity of Participants. It isn't necessary to be able-bodied or financially secure to do direct action to support clinics. Thanks to online tools and social media organizing, any person with access to a computer or phone and Internet can take part in efforts like petition creating, e-mail and text campaigns, awareness raising, and more. Newer online apps like ResistBot can help people contact government entities more easily, and allow more participation from those who are unable to organize in a physical, face-to-face setting due to work schedules, childcare, transportation issues, or disability. Be sure that if you are starting a campaign, you are working in a way that includes all supporters, such as by holding virtual, recorded meetings that are captioned and can be played when an activist is most able to tune in, making childcare available during meetings so more parenting attendees can participate, and meeting at locations that are directly accessible to those with mobility issues and those who use mass transit.

Do You Want to Get Even More Directly Involved?

Many clinics use volunteers. Some have clinic escorts to help patients navigate their way past protesters and into the clinic itself; others have volunteers who talk to patients during their procedures to help them feel relaxed and supported (abortion doulas). Others call volunteers in on days when they expect larger, specialized, one-off protests, such as on Good Friday.

Always contact your local clinic before arriving to help. Expect to be vetted in some way by the clinic, which will want to ensure its patients and staff stay safe. Then assume that you will go through a training (perhaps more than one) before you actually interact with patients.

ALWAYS follow the clinic's lead. Do not show up at the clinic until you are invited and especially do NOT take it upon yourself to "counterprotest" or hold any other activity outside a clinic without explicit consent. To patients seeking a termination, there is no difference between anti-abortion protesters and pro-choice protesters: both are there, interfering with their attempt to easily and privately access the clinic.

We will discuss how to get involved with organizations supporting abortion and clinic access in more detail in the "Finding Your Personal Cause" chapter.

How Can You Protect Access if Your State Makes Abortion Mostly or Totally Illegal?

Then, of course, there is what to do if your state makes abortion nearly or completely illegal in all cases. The good news is, things aren't as hopeless as they seem. As long as abortion is legal in the United States as a whole, there is always the possibility that abortion bans can be struck down with subsequent laws if there is enough turnover in the state legislature. Once residents of a state see the actual impact of no longer having legal abortion available, there is a strong possibility that voters and legislators will realize that total bans do far more harm than good.

Until that happens, there are some places where you can make the most impact legislatively even without legal abortion in your state.

Protect the Access That Does Still Exist

While it may not seem like it, a total or near-total state abortion ban still isn't the worst thing that could happen. The worst thing that could happen would be if there was a total ban and a person who wanted to end a pregnancy couldn't leave the state to do it.

This sort of *Handmaid's Tale* scenario doesn't seem likely for the general population, but it could easily become a reality for minors wanting to end a pregnancy. For over a decade Congress has introduced in some form a federal Child Interstate Abortion Notification Act (CIANA)—a bill that would make it illegal for anyone other than a minor's legal guardian to take that child to another state to obtain an abortion, with the adult who crosses state lines subject to criminal prosecution.

While CIANA would impact all minors seeking care, it is those who are poor and especially those who come from immigrant families who would be most affected. Many southern states have parental notification laws that require notarized birth certificates or other costly documentation to prove a familial relationship. Those who are in the country without papers may be unable to officially approve an abortion for their child even though they are legal guardians—especially now that the Trump administration is more aggressively deporting immigrants. Others may be incarcerated, too ill to travel, or unable to get off work, or they may have too many children to care for at home or other obligations. There are a myriad of reasons why another adult could need to take a minor across a state line for an abortion rather than the pregnant teen's legal guardian, but CIANA rejects all of these factors.

It would not be surprising to see some form of CIANA reintroduced now and for the bill to finally pass—especially if some states had no legal abortion at all. However, we also need to be vigilant about individual states passing their own similar laws that may equate helping a person leave the state with "procuring" an illegal abortion, especially for minors who have little ability to travel on their own.

Also be prepared for any "cleanup" of exceptions that are left in current total bans. Check to see if your state allows an exception to its abortion bans if the pregnant person's health is at risk, or if they were impregnated as a result of sexual assault. While most people—including many who identify as pro-life—believe that a person should be allowed to terminate if that person was impregnated through sexual assault, many anti-abortion groups reject that exception, primarily because they believe that people may make up rape claims in order to obtain an abortion.

Pressuring your legislators to ensure that at a minimum victims of sexual assault still have access to abortion care—and aren't forced to carry to term just because of the state they live in—is not just a reasonable action that reflects the majority's beliefs on abortion. It also offers a clear incremental step toward repealing abortion bans as a whole down the road, and it exposes just how radical the Right's position has become.

Work to Pass a Bill to Protect Those Who Experience Poor Pregnancy Outcomes

Maternal mortality and poor pregnancy outcomes are rising all across the US already, and that increase is especially concentrated among pregnant people of color. Due to poverty, lack of affordable, consistent preventive health care services including and beyond contraception, and longstanding systemic racial bias in medical care and treatment, Black and brown people are far more likely to be less healthy when they get pregnant, receive less prenatal care, and face greater risk of miscarriage, stillbirth, and premature labor.

And if *Roe* is overturned, every single instance of these poor birth outcomes could be investigated as a potential illegal abortion.

If there is just one bill to be championed in states where abortion is greatly or completely restricted, it would be the Public Leadership Institute's "Pregnant Women's Dignity Act." The model, which would be highly beneficial in both blue and red states alike, demands that law enforcement not be called in to investigate when a person miscarries or delivers a stillbirth. Even with abortion technically legal, numerous people have been arrested and prosecuted, either for allegedly inducing their own abortions, for miscarrying fetuses on the cusp of viability and not seeking medical attention in time, for miscarrying and disposing of fetal remains without alerting medical practitioners or authorities, for unfavorable birth outcomes after illicit drug use, and even for premature labor after a suicide attempt.

Once abortion is illegal ALL miscarriages will potentially be subject to questioning by the authorities, with doctors, police, and district attorneys able to decide at their own discretion what constitutes a "suspicious" circumstance that might lead to a more in-depth investigation. The Pregnant Women's Dignity Act protects all people from having their unsuccessful pregnancies scrutinized, allowing every pregnant person the same freedom in their birth outcomes.

The model bill can be found at http://publicleadershipinstitute. org/abortion-rights/pregnant-womens-dignity-act/. It is also available at www.postroehandbook.com.

Direct Action in States Where Abortion Is Illegal

It's a daunting prospect. With abortion illegal in particular states, there will be three options: getting pregnant people who want to end their pregnancies to states where they can do that, getting them the tools to end their pregnancies in their home states (as well as their literal homes), even if that means defying local laws, and supporting those who are arrested should any illegal actions be discovered and prosecuted.

Each of these options will be explored in detail in the next few chapters.

Learn the Language

Abortion opponents are especially good at changing public opinion, usually by reframing abortion rights in harmful or stigmatizing language. You'll find their words in right-wing media stories, in letters to the editor, in the comments sections of online news sites, and of course all over social media.

That leaves abortion rights supporters with the unenviable job of correcting the record. Need a little help? Here are some explanations of the Right's favorite talking points.

"Fetuses Feel Pain"

At what point is a fetus or embryo capable of feeling pain? It depends who you ask—and no, I'm not talking about doctors or mainstream medical professionals. Anti-abortion activists themselves constantly change their minds about when they believe a fetus feels pain, manipulating the dates depending on which abortion restriction they are trying to pass at the time.

Depending on which bill they are trying to promote, abortion opponents will say that a fetus can feel pain at twenty-two weeks' gestation or at fifteen weeks' gestation. The anti-abortion research group Charlotte Lozier Institute even offers a fact sheet that provides justifications for claiming fetal or embryonic pain can be felt at twenty, ten, or a mere six weeks.[28]

None of the literature cited in these reports comes from mainstream organizations like the American College of Obstetricians and Gynecologists, the American Medical Association, or the Royal College of Obstetricians and Gynaecologists. These major medical associations all agree that while the receptors necessary to eventually feel pain do develop at the points anti-abortion activists claim, the system as a whole is incapable of transmitting any pain until all structures are in place and operating—including the brain, which isn't fully developed until some point near the third trimester.[29]

"Born Alive," "Viability," and "Infanticide"

While abortion rights supporters fight in state legislatures to protect access in case *Roe* is overturned, abortion opponents claim prochoice legislators are championing "infanticide." But in order to make their argument work, anti-abortion activists often manipulate the public perception around the idea of viability.

"Viability" refers to the point at which a fetus—if delivered—would be capable of surviving outside the womb with the assistance of life support. As technology has improved, that marker has dramatically decreased, moving from around the third trimester back when *Roe* was decided in the 1970s to as early as twenty-two weeks' gestation today.

Now, viability does not mean every fetus will survive at that point in gestation. It also doesn't mean every one that does survive will do so without severe medical issues. What "viability" does do is serve as a point at which doctors who are dealing with premature labor of a wanted pregnancy can offer medical intervention for the fetus to increase chances of survival, versus knowing that providing care is futile and would only cause more harm.

That's where the Right takes advantage of the language. A fetus that is delivered at eighteen weeks has no possibility of survival. But that doesn't mean it will not be "born alive." Viability is based primarily on lung development, and a fetus's lungs prior to about twenty-two weeks' gestation lack the surfactant necessary for them to inflate and deflate without tears or collapse. The production of this surfactant begins at around twenty weeks, and can be accelerated with medication once it starts, but it cannot be produced prior to twenty weeks.

Abortion opponents will tell stories in Congress, in state Houses, in television interviews and campaign commercials about "babies born alive and left gasping rather than being offered medical care." But the reality is that providing oxygen to a fetus whose lungs are not yet able to inflate and deflate will do nothing other than cause more harm. But when doctors don't provide medical care, the Right then accuses them of promoting "infanticide."

The simple truth is there is no clear line for viability. It differs for every fetus, based on prenatal health, genetics, gestational age, weight, and even gender. But nuance is hard to debate, and abortion opponents rely on that fact in order to manipulate public perception.

"Taxpayer-Funded Abortion"

It used to be that the idea of "taxpayer-funded abortion" was relegated to the Hyde Amendment, which originally forbade people on Medicaid from using their insurance to pay for an abortion. But now this phrase has been expanded to encompass any situation where a person could claim that taxes are being used to pay for something related to an abortion.

The Helms Amendment, a companion to Hyde, forbids any

person who is in the military or who gets their medical care through military services from being able to obtain an abortion—it even blocks military bases from providing abortions. This has a devastating effect on military families, especially those who may be deployed overseas and into countries where abortion is difficult to find or outright illegal.

But Hyde has also been used to block those who work for the government from using their insurance to pay for abortions, effectively stopping government employees, city employees, and others from having the procedure covered. And during the 2009 battle over the Affordable Health Act, Hyde was used to stop insurance plans on the state and federal health exchanges from covering abortion. While a handful of states made it mandatory for all plans offered in their state exchanges to cover reproductive health care, regardless of the type, Republicans not only sought to block abortion coverage for most states but also sued to ensure there was at least one insurance plan in every state that didn't cover abortion.

Insurance coverage isn't the only area where the Far Right makes overzealous claims of "taxpayer-funded abortion." Conservatives have created increasingly convoluted claims of "fungible funding" to argue that taxpayers are financially supporting abortion services by providing Title X funding (federal funds to support birth control for low income and uninsured individuals) to Planned Parenthood affiliates. These accusations escalated since 2010, despite the fact that the organization has been required for decades to produce reports proving their contraceptive programs are kept separate from any abortion services.

To eliminate any possibility of "taxpayer-funded" abortion, the Trump administration passed a new rule in early 2019 that forbids any entity that is associated with, recommends, or even mentions abortion from receiving any Title X funding. This "ultra gag rule" was introduced under the guise that any rent, utility bill, band-aid, or photocopy subsidized by the government somehow frees up a dollar that could then be used for an abortion. By demanding entities that discuss or offer abortion have complete physical separation from any clinic given funding for contraception, conservatives argued that only that complete isolation of Title X funding could guarantee not one dollar inadvertently "funded" an abortion.

If that isn't a big enough stretch, the "taxpayer-funded" abortion trope is used in the same way to stop abortion providers from being able to operate in states that require medically unnecessary admitting privileges or transfer agreements in order to maintain a license.

One example is Ohio, where legislature passed a law requiring all abortion clinics to have local admitting privileges with a nearby hospital. Unsurprisingly, many hospitals refused to offer privileges because they were religious-based institutions that "morally" objected to the procedure. But the state next made a rule that public and university hospitals could not offer transfer agreements either, because they were subsidized with tax funding. Providing a transfer agreement that would allow abortion clinics to operate—the state theorized—would then be taxpayer funding of abortion. Clinics were left with only one option: finding a local, non-religious, non–publicly funded hospital that would work with them.

Prior to these rules, Ohio had nearly twenty clinics. Today, they have eight.

Taxpayers will always be forced to fund programs they disagree with. Taxes fund wars, jails, bailouts for the rich, stadiums and sports arenas and all sorts of programs many oppose. Yet somehow a moral objection by a minority of Americans to the legal act of terminating a pregnancy has become an issue so sacrosanct that abortions has been removed line by line from the entire US tax code. That's not a reasonable moral objection, that's weaponizing a political view.

Chapter 4 Worksheet
Checklist for Political Engagement

1) *Get registered to vote.*
   a) See if your community allows mail-in ballots.
   b) Find your races and candidates at www.voteprochoice.us.
   c) Find a local reproductive rights organization or pick a candidate and offer to phone bank or otherwise get out the vote.
2) Get to know your city council.
   a) Learn your council members, when they meet, and see if you can find their agenda.
   b) Many local meetings are streamed live; see if you can find yours.
   c) Consider offering a pro-choice resolution (see model legislation at www.postroehandbook.com).
3) Speak out.
   a) Make a list of your local media outlets.
   b) Write a response to any anti-abortion op-eds or letters you see.
   c) Draft your own pro-choice op-ed or letter to the editor.

Tips for Letters, from the ACLU:[30]

1) Keep your letter short and to the subject.
2) Send to weekly community newspapers as well as mainstream publications.
3) Make references to the article or letter you are responding to.
4) Include your contact information.

Finding Your Personal Cause

It's completely understandable if your first reaction to the unraveling of abortion rights is to want to give all of your money to pro-choice organizations, convert your spare bedroom into an abortion Airbnb, buy out your local pharmacy's stock of Plan B, or even start researching how to make a manual vacuum aspirator.

Take a minute and pause. You don't have to do everything yourself, and a lot of activists have been planning for this moment for decades. The bad news is that abortion is now going to be mostly or completely illegal in many states. The good news is that national and local organizations—especially reproductive justice groups—have been on the ground for decades preparing for this possibility. They were doing the heavy lifting on reproductive rights and access issues while most of the privileged population of America was content to believe that abortion was a "settled issue" and *Roe* would never be overturned.

Rather than replicate efforts, look first to these groups and find out how you can best support those who already have their networks in place.

National Network of Abortion Funds

The National Network of Abortion Funds (NNAF) is an organization encompassing member funds in nearly every state in the nation. NNAF provides policy support, technical support, fund-raising support, and other resources to member funds while fighting against abortion-funding bans and other restrictions that make it more difficult for pregnant people to access legal abortion care. They also work to center the needs of people of color and other marginalized communities in their advocacy, since those are the groups in the most need and who face the greatest risks if they cannot access care.

NNAF acts as the national clearing-house for regional, state, and city-based funds and affiliates, which can all be found at https://abortionfunds.org/need-abortion/#funds. NNAF also offers a personal membership option as well. By becoming an individual member, you are not just providing financial support to NNAF, you will also receive monthly news updates about abortion access, including actions that you may be able to participate in and net-working opportunities with your regional fund.

You can join NNAF as an individual member at https://nnaf.formstack.com/forms/membership, or call 617-267-7161.

National and State Reproductive Rights Organizations

NARAL Pro-Choice America and State Affiliates

NARAL Pro-Choice America existed before *Roe*, and it will prob-ably be there long after *Roe* is gone. As one of the first organizations to publicly lobby for abortion law reform and repeal, NARAL networks across the country to keep abortion legal. The national NARAL group can be reached at:

NARAL Pro-Choice America
1156 15th St. NW, Suite 700. Washington, DC 20005
202-973-3000
https://www.prochoiceamerica.org/

The following states have local branches where you can assist in on-the-ground work like funding, canvassing, lobbying, and more.

CALIFORNIA

NARAL Pro-Choice California
335 S. Van Ness Ave., San Francisco, CA 94103
415-890-1020
https://prochoicecalifornia.org/
info@prochoicecalifornia.org

CONNECTICUT

NARAL Pro-Choice Connecticut
1 Main St., Suite T4, Hartford, CT 06106
203-787-8763
https://www.prochoicect.org
info@prochoicect.org

GEORGIA

NARAL Pro-Choice Georgia
202-973-3000
https://prochoicegeorgia.org/
georgia@prochoiceamerica.org

ILLINOIS

Illinois Choice Action Team
1333 W. Devon Ave. #253, Chicago, IL 60660
312-458-9169
https://www.ilchoiceactionteam.org/
info@ilchoiceactionteam.org

IOWA

NARAL Pro-Choice Iowa
https://prochoiceiowa.org/
iowa@prochoiceamerica.org

MARYLAND

NARAL Pro-Choice Maryland
8905 Fairview Rd., Suite 401, Silver Spring, MD 20910
301-565-4154
https://prochoicemd.org/
info@prochoicemd.org

MASSACHUSETTS

NARAL Pro-Choice Massachusetts
15 Court Sq., Suite 900, Boston, MA 02108-2524
617-556-8800
https://prochoicemass.org/
choice@prochoicemass.org

MINNESOTA

NARAL Pro-Choice Minnesota
2300 Myrtle Ave., Suite 120, Saint Paul, MN 55114
651-602-765
https://prochoiceminnesota.org/
info@prochoiceminnesota.org

MISSOURI

NARAL Pro-Choice Missouri
1210 S. Vandeventer Ave., St. Louis, MO 63110
314-531-8616
https://prochoicemissouri.org/
naral@prochoicemissouri.org

MONTANA

NARAL Pro-Choice Montana
PO Box 279, Helena, MT 59624
406-813-1680
https://www.prochoicemontana.org/
npmtinterim@gmail.com

NEVADA

NARAL Pro-Choice Nevada
702-751-4219
https://prochoicenevada.org/
nevada@prochoiceamerica.org

NORTH CAROLINA

NARAL Pro-Choice North Carolina
4711 Hope Valley Rd., Suite 4F-509, Durham, NC 27702
919-908-9321
https://prochoicenc.org/
info@prochoicenc.org

OHIO

NARAL Pro-Choice Ohio
12000 Shaker Blvd., Cleveland, OH 44120
216-283-2180
https://prochoiceohio.org/

OREGON

NARAL Pro-Choice Oregon
PO Box 40472, Portland, OR 97240
503-223-4510
https://prochoiceoregon.org/
info@prochoiceoregon.org

TEXAS

NARAL Pro-Choice Texas
PO Box 684602, Austin, TX 78768
512-462-1661
http://prochoicetexas.org/
info@prochoicetexas.org

VIRGINIA

NARAL Pro-Choice Virginia
PO Box 1204, Alexandria, VA 22313-1204
571-970-2536
https://naralva.org/
info@naralva.org

WASHINGTON

NARAL Pro-Choice Washington
811 First Ave., Suite 675, Seattle, WA 98104
206-624-1990
https://prochoicewashington.org/
info@prochoicewashington.org

WISCONSIN

NARAL Pro-Choice Wisconsin
612 W. Main St. #200, Madison, WI 53703
608-287-0016
info@prochoicewisconsin.org

WYOMING

NARAL Pro-Choice Wyoming
PO Box 271, Laramie, WY 82073
307-742-9189
https://prochoicewyoming.org/
naralprochoicewy@netscape.net

Planned Parenthood Action Fund

As the state and federal governments increase their attacks not just on abortion but on birth control access, too, Planned Parenthood Federation of America has increased its own action fund to organize against political attacks. A number of states have Planned Parenthood health care centers as their primary source of contraception and STI testing and treatment for those who are uninsured or underinsured. If you are looking for a direct way to politically support Planned Parenthood by lobbying or otherwise doing advocacy in your state, contact the national Planned Parenthood Action Fund (PPFA), and they will get you connected to your local affiliate. The individual state action funds are also listed in the "State Resources" section of the Resource Guide.

PPAF's national offices are located in DC and New York City:

1110 Vermont Ave. NW, Washington, DC 20005
Phone: 202-973-4800

123 William St., 10th Floor, New York, NY 10038
Phone: 212-541-7800

actionfund@ppfa.org

Abortion Access Front and Abortion Access Force (AAF)

Founded by comedienne Lizz Winstead, AAF (formerly Lady Parts Justice) battles the right wing with humor. AAF undertakes state and local campaigns to increase voter outreach, support local independent clinics with practical and financial support for special projects, and perform awareness-raising activities across the nation. Abortion Access Front is the 501(c)3 non-profit, while Abortion Access

Force is a (c)4 that does political work. Abortion Access Front has spearheaded the "Keep Our Clinics Open" campaign to financially support independent abortion providers across the country. They also provide on-the-ground listings for clinic support, resources for protesting at anti-abortion rallies and events, and information on anti-abortion activists on both a local and national level.

https://www.aafront.org/
https://www.aaforce.org
Donations: https://www.aafront.org/donate/ *or* https://www.aafront.org/join-us/

Storytelling Projects and Art

One in four people who can get pregnant will have an abortion at some point in their lives, and yet our society remains solidly afraid of talking candidly and explicitly about real abortion experiences. For decades anti-abortion activists speaking out about their regrets have been the only ones to publicly talk about abortion.

Storytelling projects are breaking down the stigma surrounding abortion, helping people better understand that there aren't "good" abortions or "bad" abortions, that every abortion is an individual experience and just as valid as anyone else's.

"We Testify," "Shout Your Abortion," Abortion Conversation Project, and The Abortion Diary all use different tactics to break down the silence and stigma around abortion, from empowering storytellers to talk to lawmakers, to engaging social media users to talk about their own experiences in more public ways, to funding projects meant to end the silence and shame society wraps around the procedure and the people who obtain it.

We Testify

https://wetestify.org/
https://wetestify.org/testify/

Shout Your Abortion

https://shoutyourabortion.com/
ShoutYourAbortion@gmail.com

Abortion Conversation Project

http://www.abortionconversationproject.org/
abortionconversation@gmail.com

The Abortion Diary

https://www.theabortiondiary.com/

Art, too, has become a means of breaking down abortion stigma and is especially important in a landscape where there isn't one clear symbol that is universally recognized as an icon of the pro-choice movement. Artists like Heather Ault of 4000 Years for Choice and Megan Smith of Repeal Hyde Art Project are working to change that by introducing new visual images that better represent the history, diversity, complexity, and strength that comes with embracing bodily autonomy.

4000 Years for Choice

https://www.4000yearsforchoice.com/
https://www.4000yearsforchoice.com/pages/contact

Repeal Hyde Art Project

http://www.repealhydeartproject.org/
megan@repealhydeartproject.org

All-Options Pregnancy Centers

The Right may love to call us "pro-abortion," but let's be clear, we are "pro-abortion" only in the fact that we believe anyone who wants an abortion to be able to access one safely and easily without hurdles, roadblocks, or waits. But the last thing we want is for a person who really wants to stay pregnant and give birth to find themselves seeking out an abortion because they don't feel they have the resources they need to make it through the pregnancy.

Pregnancy centers do serve an important role in our society, offering financial, material, and governmental support to people who want to give birth and don't have everything they need. Unfortunately, pregnancy centers are almost exclusively a tool of abortion opponents seeking to convince someone not to end a pregnancy, and as such offer medically biased and sometimes outright false information. Anti-abortion pregnancy centers will try to trick or coerce people into giving birth when they do decide they want an abortion, imposing their choice on the person who is pregnant. And then, in many cases, they rip that assistance away shortly after the birth, or within a few months, claiming they are trying to help that person not develop a "cycle of dependency" on outside help.[31]

But pregnancy centers don't have to be coercive, or political. In Indiana, All-Options Pregnancy Center offers counseling to those who are truly conflicted about their unplanned pregnancy. They advise on the pros and cons of abortion, birth, parenting, and adoption, holding no choice as more valid than another and offering resources and support for each option if the person wants it. They recognize that the person who is pregnant and considering an abortion today may be a person who already gave birth, or who will give birth in the future under different circumstances, or someone who had an abortion in the past and wants to consider different options this time. They believe people who give birth and people who have abortions are all the same people, just at different stages of their lives.

To learn more about All Options Pregnancy Resource Center, go to https://alloptionsprc.org/, or call 812-558-0089.

They also have a wish list of items that can be easily sent to their location:

- Diapers (sizes 4, 5, 6)
- Pull-ups/training pants 4T/5T
- Wipes (fragrance-free)
- Hot/cold packs
- Baby blankets
- Feminine hygiene products
- Diaper rash ointment
- Baby powder
- Baby lotion
- Condoms
- Wet bags for cloth diapers
- Hats and gloves for babies/children
- Individually wrapped chocolates (for care kits)
- Baby boxes

Gifts and donations can be sent to their physical address at 1014 Walnut St., Bloomington, IN 47401.

We need more of these nonjudgmental, secular resources outside the bounds and rules of the religious Right. Supporting All Options is just the first step in getting there.

Abortion Funding

Pre- or post-*Roe*, with legal abortion in every state or without it, funding abortions is going to be the absolute most important thing you can do to keep the procedure accessible. Luckily, it's also one of the easiest things you can do.

According to the Guttmacher Institute, as of 2014 about 75 percent of those who seek abortions are low-income, making abortion costs a major hardship financially—one that many are unable to cover without outside assistance.[32] Because such a large proportion of those who are low-income are also people of color, the inability to obtain an abortion because of financial needs isn't just an economics issue but a racial justice issue, too.

When it comes to making sure that people can afford the procedure, a good first stop is When it comes to making sure that people can afford the procedure, a good first stop is your local abortion fund. You can find them either by using NNAF's state guide at https://abortionfunds.org/need-abortion/#funds-list or by googling (State Name) + "abortion fund," which will provide you with additional and equally valid options that may not be under the NNAF umbrella.

State and Regional Funds

Funding abortions can also start literally at your front door. There are funds in nearly every state that help provide either for those having an abortion at a clinic in the state, or for those from that state who need to travel elsewhere for care.

Not all funds function in the same way. Some funds are places patients should contact directly to get assistance, and the fund will work with the clinic. Other funds are ones where the patient contacts the clinic, and the clinic will then contact the fund. Some funds will also provide financial support for costs related to obtaining the abortion, or arrange for additional needs like lodging or travel, providing practical support aspects, too. Others work with specific practical support groups outside their fund. Patients should be sure to understand what the fund can and can't provide and who will initiate the contact with the fund—the patient or the clinic. All funds are in desperate need of more financial support from donors and more volunteers to work their hotlines.

How Should You Donate?

If you have a chunk of change you want to donate, go right ahead and do it—every fund would be more than grateful for the support. But while one donation is a huge help, recurring donations are even better since they help these organizations plan for expenses coming down the road, too, and let them know that even if the fund goes dry in August, September means a fresh start.

If you have the financial ability, consider becoming a monthly donor. A five- or ten-dollar-a-month donation may hardly be noticeable in your account, but being able to rely on it doesn't just help organizers plan ahead, it saves them the resources needed to fundraise if they run out of money down the road. As one activist on Twitter suggested just after Justice Kennedy announced his retirement, if churches can rely on people to give 10 percent of their income in tithes, shouldn't those who support reproductive rights and have the financial means consider doing something similar for abortion funds?

Donating Things Other Than Money (Gas Cards, Restaurant Cards, and Other Gifts)

Gas cards are one of the best items to donate to any group that assists abortion patients. While abortion funds tend to help primarily with payment for the procedure itself (often working directly with a clinic to ensure the procedure is paid for), there are a large number of incidentals that may not end up in the initial cost that can still create barriers to getting the abortion itself.

Cards to gas stations can be especially useful, as they not only can be used to close the gap in travel expenses (especially for patients who are forced to drive to a clinic twice due to mandatory in-person waiting periods of twenty-four to seventy-two hours, or those who need to leave the state in order to get an appointment at all), but they can also be used to purchase food, drink, painkillers, sanitary pads, and other necessities while a patient is away from home.

"We like to do gas card drives," explained Meg Stern, a reproductive justice activist and support fund director at Kentucky Health Justice Network. "We ask donors to buy Kroger cards, or prepaid credit cards when they shop. It's an easy way for them to make an impact, especially if they accumulate points for buying cards."

You can also purchase restaurant gift cards to give to local groups for the patients they are assisting. Ask whichever organization you are supporting which restaurants are closest to the clinics or the hotels where patients may be staying, and especially focus on places that offer delivery so an abortion patient doesn't need to put any more effort into traveling than necessary.

Cards for gas, restaurants, even hotels can all be obtained at discounts if you use customer loyalty programs, and also if you transfer credit card points to purchase them. If you are looking for the best way to use these loyalty or rewards programs to benefit someone trying to access abortion, contact a fund or your local reproductive rights or reproductive justice organization and ask them exactly what they need (food cards, gas cards, hotel rooms), then address those specific requests.

Of course, some people will be traveling from other states, or from rural areas, and in their cases a Holiday gas card or a certificate to Domino's for a delivery doesn't do much good because those vendors aren't out there. In those cases, Stern says, her group offers Visa cards instead.

While some may be uncomfortable with the idea of essentially offering straight cash to a patient, the reality is that these cards provide the most flexibility, allowing a patient to pay a sitter or family member who is watching their children or maybe pay a bill they had to put off for a month to have enough money to pay for the procedure, among other things. "We aren't trying to be gatekeepers," Stern said. "The more power we can put into the patients' hands, the better."

Stern notes, however, that because Visa cards have a surcharge attached, their group is more likely to purchase other cards.

Donating Miles and Hotel Points

At this point, there isn't really an easy way to donate airline miles in order to help a person fly to a clinic for an abortion. Every airline has its own specific frequent flier program, and while some do offer ways to pool miles (either various people into one pool, or various airlines into one pool for one individual), the actual transfer of miles tends to be an expensive process. If you want to dedicate miles, consider contacting your local abortion fund or practical support group for suggestions.

Hotel points and loyalty programs for lodging also come with the same roadblocks when it comes to donations. If you are still invested in finding a way to give hotel points to people who may need to stay overnight near a clinic, again, talk to a local fund, a practical support group, or a local reproductive justice or rights group about which hotels are most likely to be used and how you can directly assist.

Practical Support Groups

There is a distinct difference between an abortion fund and a practical support group, although there are a number of funding groups that provide practical support as well as part of their case management.

For the most part, abortion funds exist to help those who need an abortion find the financial resources to cover the expenses (the procedure, gas, hotel if necessary, and so on). Some work directly with the clinics to find funding, others directly with the patients to meet their needs.

A practical support group, on the other hand, may do abortion funding, but much of their mission is to handle the nonprocedural needs of patients, such as providing transportation to a clinic or a place to stay if the patient needs to remain in town overnight, or making sure meals are delivered to the patient's hotel or home so the patient can rest, or even finding childcare so the patient can make it to a multihour appointment. Practical support groups are also a lifeline for patients with language barriers or disabilities, providing translation services and additional physical support, and ensuring that those who need accessible clinic entrances or transportation can get them. Practical support is also a necessary part of aiding minors navigating the abortion process, from helping them get to clinics to handling judicial bypass in parental-notification-and-consent states.

While abortion funding already exists in many states, the practical support networks needed to help patients overcome the additional roadblocks besides just paying for an abortion aren't nearly as prevalent. Practical support networks were thrust into the media more prominently starting in 2014 as the Texas Omnibus Abortion Bill was put into effect, at one point closing more than half the clinics in the state and leaving the remainder located in just five large urban areas. The Cicada Collective, which had formed in April 2013, began the very public work of arranging travel for Texas patients trying to get to the closest clinic for care, a job that conservative media derisively called "abortion vacations," as if Texans were jaunting off for a weekend on the beach.

Since then, practical support networks and organizations have emerged across the country, as a critical response to the myriad and increasing barriers that impact how someone is able to safely get to their abortion. Practical support organizations address these issues by providing some or all of the following support: arranging or covering the cost of logistics like transportation and hotels; providing stipends for meals, gas, medications, pads and other related expenses; training and coordinating volunteers to drive folks to their appointments, host them overnight, drop meals or groceries, or be a designated escort; arranging or reimbursing for the costs of childcare; and some also provide procedure funding support. Typically operating within specific locales or regions, these organizations vary in their service offerings and structure in order to fit the practical needs identified by abortion seekers, advocates, and clinics themselves. Some are volunteer based, staff-based or a mixture of the two and many exist separate from or within other organizations. This growing network has been tasked with becoming rapid responders in the face of state bans, clinic closures, hurricanes and, in 2020, a pandemic. These experiences have encouraged such organizations to be innovative and collaborative in how they move past barriers and network with one another and abortion funds along the way, streamlining the multiple needs of an abortion seeker. The effect of practical support and the following organizations is that people are increasingly able to get to their care, with less disruption to their lives, and are alleviated of much of the financial, logistical and emotional stress they'd otherwise face.

Providing multi-state support is Midwest Access Coalition, which works to get abortion seekers in the Midwestern, and some Southern, states to available abortion clinics. The Midwest's limited number of clinics, lack of later abortion providers, long waiting periods and other onerous restrictions often force patients to leave their own cities or even states, seeking out care primarily in Illinois, Minnesota, and Ohio. Highly collaborative with their provider-partners, MAC provides cash boxes near clinic locations for their staff to use for patients who need immediate access to money for their expenses. Their model of one on one client accompaniment not only provides the funding for and coordination of logistical solutions to the many barriers, but also emotional support to abortion seekers, who are often alone, throughout their entire journey.

The Brigid Alliance is a nationwide practical support organization that accompanies people who must travel long distances for later abortion care (second or third trimester care). Brigid works with their clients wherever they live to support them in traveling, on average 1,200 miles, to get to the few clinics and hospitals in the country that provide this specialized care. As later abortion care is some of the most inaccessible, stigmatized and logistically complex, this organization aims to center the needs of its clients and provider-partners by providing customizable, one-on-one support through its trained staff coordinators and by working in deep collaboration with local and regional networks, doula collectives and funds across the country.

Brigid Alliance can be found at

https://brigidalliance.org/
info@brigidalliance.org

and Midwest Access Coalition (MAC) at

847-750-6224
https://midwestaccesscoalition.org/
info@midwestaccesscoalition.org

Other practical support groups doing work within their specific regions are:

Southeast

P.O.W.E.R. HOUSE (MONTGOMERY, ALABAMA)

Run by the Montgomery Area Reproductive Justice Coalition, the P.O.W.E.R. House can be used by the patients of Reproductive Health Services of Montgomery and their companions. It offers shelter, a night's stay with enough notice, and a place for a patient's support person to wait with children if they have been brought to town for the appointment.

https://montgomeryareareproductivejusticecoalition.wordpress.com/
montgomeryareareprojustice@gmail.com

NEW ORLEANS ABORTION FUND (LOUISIANA)

The New Orleans Abortion Fund can provide funding for gas,

car rentals, and hotels for those coming to the state or needing to leave the state in order to get abortion care more quickly.

https://www.neworleansabortionfund.org/get-help
504-363-1112

ACCESS REPRODUCTIVE CARE SOUTHEAST (ARC SOUTHEAST)

Serving patients in Alabama, Florida, Georgia, Mississippi, South Carolina, and Tennessee, ARC can help arrange rides to clinics, escorts to an appointment, or lodging near abortion clinics throughout the Southeast.

855-227-2475
https://www.arc-southeast.org/
Or contact them via their support request page at https://www.arc-southeast.org/
   assistance-form.

ARKANSAS ABORTION SUPPORT NETWORK (AASN) (LITTLE ROCK)

AASN is able to provide limited rides to the state's abortion providers in Little Rock.

501-712-0671
https://www.araborionsupport.org

Texas

FUND TEXAS CHOICE

This organization helps cover transportation and lodging expenses for those who need to travel to access an abortion in Texas or for Texans accessing care outside the state. This includes bus and airplane tickets as well as hotel rooms and other necessities. This group serves all of Texas.

844-900-8908
https://fundtexaschoice.org/

BRIDGE COLLECTIVE (AUSTIN)

Bridge provides transportation and lodging specifically for patients using Austin-area clinics. Lodging is often provided in the homes of their volunteers. Volunteers have all been trained and vetted by the group to ensure safety.

512-524-9822
https://thebridgecollective.org/STANDinfo

CICADA COLLECTIVE (DALLAS/FORT WORTH)

This group provides practical support such as lodging, transportation, and abortion doulas to North Texas abortion clinics.

940-441-3337
http://www.cicadacollective.org/ntx-abortion-support-network-ntx-asn.html
ntx.asn@gmail.com

CLINIC ACCESS SUPPORT NETWORK (CASN) (HOUSTON)

Like the others, CASN provides practical support like rides and overnight lodging for patients coming to Houston-area abortion clinics.

281-947-2276
http://clinicaccess.org/index.html

FRONTERA FUND (RIO GRANDE VALLEY)

The Frontera Fund specifically assists those in the Rio Grande Valley, either those seeking an abortion in the valley or those trying to travel from the valley to other clinics. The group primarily provides financial support to cover hotel costs for these patients.

956-307-9330
https://lafronterafund.org/

Southwest

NEW MEXICO RELIGIOUS COALITION FOR REPRODUCTIVE CHOICE (ALBUQUERQUE)

Home to one of only a few third-trimester providers in the country, the city of Albuquerque often sees many out-of-state patients. The New Mexico Religious Coalition for Reproductive Choice provides food, lodging, and transportation to those in need of services to make that trip a little easier.

http://nmrcrc.org/if-you-are-pregnant/financial-assistance/
officeassistant@nmrcrc.org
(Note: please attempt to use the secure request form found on the financial assistance
    page before trying to contact the group via e-mail.)

West Coast

NORTHWEST ABORTION ACCESS FUND (NWAAF) (NORTHWEST AND HAWAII)

Set up specifically for those in the Pacific Northwest, NWAAF's travel support program will help arrange transportation and patient stays in local homes to help make an abortion more accessible. NWAAF funds those in Washington, Oregon, Idaho, and Alaska.

866-692-2310, ext. 3
https://nwaafund.org/travelhelp/

CASCADES ABORTION SUPPORT COLLECTIVE (OREGON)

Located in Oregon, this group provides abortion doulas for support during procedures, as well as transportation to clinics in Portland, Oregon, and Vancouver, Washington.

503-610-0692
http://www.cascadesabortionsupport.org/
cascadesabortiondoulas@gmail.com

ACCESS WOMEN'S HEALTH JUSTICE (CALIFORNIA)
Access will provide transportation and lodging for those who may need to travel within California in order to access an abortion clinic.

800-376-4636 (English); 888-442-2237 (Spanish)
https://accesswhj.org/how-access-can-help

Midwest/Rust Belt

KENTUCKY HEALTH JUSTICE NETWORK
This Louisville organization coordinates support needs for those heading into Kentucky from neighboring states or those who may need to leave the state in order to access care.

855-576-4576
http://www.kentuckyhealthjusticenetwork.org/
info@khjn.org

East Coast

HAVEN COALITION (NEW YORK)
Haven Coalition offers lodging and personal escorts to and from abortion clinics in all five boroughs of New York City.

http://www.havencoalition.org/
havencoalition@gmail.com

Abortion Doulas

Abortion doulas, much like abortion itself, have existed since the beginning of history in the form of wise women, midwives, and healers. Today, abortion doulas are often enlisted to assist patients who are undergoing aspiration or other procedural abortion services at clinics, holding hands, providing emotional support, and generally assisting a pregnant person in the same way a doula assists pregnant people giving birth.

"Like with most medical procedures, friends and family aren't allowed to accompany a patient during the actual abortion," doula Augusta MacQueen explained in a June 2017 article in *Self* magazine. "But some patients want support, like a hand to hold or someone to joke with and distract them during the procedure. Or, someone to be with them emotionally before and after, to listen and hold space for them to express what they feel. That's where abortion doulas come in—we can offer free support to abortion patients throughout their time at the clinic."[33]

Doulas provide support inside clinics, but there are also abortion doulas who work independently of medical providers, offering assistance to those who have chosen to undergo a medication abortion outside a clinic. Because medication abortion is a much longer and often more intense experience, these doulas may come to a patient's home, or be available via phone call, text, or video chat, in order to calm, encourage, or otherwise assist a patient who is managing their miscarriage, answering questions about bleeding or pain management, helping a patient feel connected and cared for during the abortion.

Doulas will often agree to assist during a medication abortion regardless of whether the patient has obtained medication through a clinic, doctor, telemedicine appointment, online pharmacy, or other source, without judgment or shame. However, please remember that many states consider it a crime to obtain medication and induce a miscarriage outside a legal clinic setting. If a person is hoping for support during a self-managed abortion that could be considered illegal, that person would need to be very careful about reaching out to a doula, and their safest choices would be from a vetted doula network.

Some local and national doula groups are:

CICADA COLLECTIVE (AZ)
Abortion doula support for Arizona.

http://www.cicadacollective.org/

BAY AREA DOULA PROJECT (CA)
Full-spectrum doulas in Northern California dedicated to those who are choosing abortion, offering "unconditional support to women in need."

http://bayareadoulaproject.org/

COLORADO DOULA PROJECT (CO)
Provides free logistical and emotional support for people accessing abortion in Colorado.

https://www.coloradodoulaproject.org/home

LOUISVILLE DOULA PROJECT (KY)
Kentucky's "radical, all volunteer grassroots doula collective."

https://www.louisvilledoulaproject.org/

CHOICES DOULA COLLECTIVE (TN)
Doulas working with the full-spectrum reproductive health care clinic at CHOICES in Memphis, Tennessee.

https://memphischoices.org/

SPIRAL COLLECTIVE (MN)

Provides transportation and emotional support for Minnesotans seeking abortion.

https://www.spiralmn.com/

THE DOULA PROJECT (NY)

A group of full-spectrum doulas who offer abortion doula services. Their services are free to anyone in New York City.

https://www.doulaproject.net/

WISE COMMUNITY DOULAS (NC)

Full-spectrum doula support for Women of Color.

https://wisecommunitydoulas.wixsite.com/wisecommunitydoulas/about_us

RESTORING OUR OWN THROUGH TRANSFORMATION (ROOTT) (OH)

Providing abortion doula services out of Columbus, Ohio.

https://www.roott.org/

CASCADES ABORTION SUPPORT COLLECTIVE (OR/WA)

Abortion support and doula organization for Portland, Oregon, and Vancouver, Washington.

https://cascadesabortionsupport.org/

BRIDGE COLLECTIVE (TX)

Support for those seeking an abortion, including doula support.

https://thebridgecollective.org/

CICADA COLLECTIVE (TX)
Abortion doula support for North Texas.

http://www.cicadacollective.org/

RICHMOND DOULA PROJECT (VA)
Providing abortion doula support to those in Richmond, Virginia.

https://doulaprojectrva.org/

PREGNANCY OPTIONS WISCONSIN (WI)
Full-spectrum doula support for the state of Wisconsin.

https://www.pregnancyoptionswi.org/doulas

What About the "Aunties"?

When state after state began introducing extreme anti-abortion legislation in 2019, strangers took to Facebook, Twitter, and Reddit, proclaiming that regardless of whether or not it could eventually get them into legal trouble, they would be willing to house, drive, or otherwise assist a person who needed an abortion but could not get one legally in their home state. Declaring themselves "aunties," these people offered bedrooms, car keys, whatever a person might need in order to travel under the guise of "visiting an aunt" in a state that had more accessible care.

While no doubt well meaning, these networks of strangers were impossible to vet. This is an even bigger concern when it comes to protecting privacy, as abortion opponents have grown more adept at inserting themselves into these spaces and harassing or derailing patients seeking support.

For someone who is truly desperate to obtain an abortion, there may be a point when meeting a stranger to get care is the only option available. But for now, thanks to these robust, trained, and highly secure abortion funds and practical support networks, there is simply no need to take a stranger up on an offer to use their spare room or accept a ride to a clinic.

If you wish to be a volunteer, please consider reaching out to these already established groups, which always need more members. We will talk more about safety, privacy, and legal protections vis-à-vis abortion care and the Internet—including online abortion support groups—in chapter 10.

Additional Support for Those Attempting Self-Managed Abortion Care Outside a Legal Clinic Setting

Self-managed abortion outside the traditional medical system currently isn't legal in the United States, but that hasn't stopped those who either cannot or choose not to access a clinic or medical provider from inducing their own abortions, either through medications obtained online or through other sources, or via herbs or other methods. To help address those who are already determined to self-induce, Women Help Women launched Self-Managed Abortion: Safe and Supported, an informational website on World Health Organization protocols for self-induction and a help line for those who may be considering self-managed care, staffed by English- and Spanish-speaking advocates from overseas.

financial backing needed for vetted overnight stays would be better spent on hotels for patients, which would both be safer and provide more autonomy for the person undergoing the procedure. However, there are practical support groups who do this sort of work directly and personally, and find it extremely helpful for patients in need.

If you are interested in offering your room or home to a person needing an overnight stay in order to get an abortion, contact your state abortion fund or reproductive rights organization to discuss the possibility. But before doing so, here are a few things to consider:

1) *Will you be providing privacy or support?* Some patients—especially those who may be staying for longer procedures—may need a host who can also bring them food, drive them to the appointment and back, or pick up medications or other items. Others may want to be left completely alone and not have any interaction with another human. Can you meet both of those needs, depending on what the guest wants? If the person wants privacy, are you able to provide a completely private space, or are there shared spaces you can't avoid?

2) *How available will your space be?* Are you going to always have an empty room, or is it just a few times a month or year? Is this a set schedule, or does it change randomly? The more work a support group needs to put into using your space for patients, the fewer resources they have for other support work.

3) *Is the space accessible?* Can it be easily accessed by wheelchair or walker? Is the bathroom wide and easy to use? Are there stairs? Is the bed high? Is there parking? If you are going to offer your home or property, you need to be sure it will meet the needs of anyone who may use it.

4) *Are you concerned about damage?* Offering a space to stay isn't like operating an Airbnb. Patients who have had abortions will

have some bleeding, and there may be other health or medical needs to address too. Also, some may need to bring family, especially young children. Be prepared to childproof, and know that breakage may very well happen regardless.

If you have concerns about any of the above, consider a different way to help, including renting out the space now and giving the proceeds to a local support group to allow them to rent hotel rooms more easily.

Thinking Big. Really Big.

Of course, in an ideal world, we could put the infrastructure in place to offer all sorts of assistance to people who need to travel for abortion care. Much as abortion opponents have purchased properties adjacent to abortion clinics in order to set up their crisis pregnancy centers, with enough financial backing practical support groups could purchase buildings that are strategically placed for maximum impact—perhaps even former abortion clinics themselves.

These "abortion hostels" would offer office space for the organization to work out of, as well as a few bedrooms to be used by patients in need. Patients could leave their children in an open common area to be watched by volunteers while they are at the clinics. Finally, a kitchen area would offer a centralized place to prepare meals for patients either staying in the hostel or nearby to help them reduce extraneous costs associated with the procedure.

"Abortion hostels" could also exist in cities where there is no clinic to serve as a gathering point for patients out in the vast landscape of states that will no longer have legal abortion. A hostel in Little Rock, for example, could act as a place for those in surrounding areas to join up and commute together to a clinic in Illinois, with the hostel hosting a passenger van or bus for patients, reducing travel costs like gas or bus tickets and providing the opportunity for patients to travel through the night in order to be at the clinic early for a procedure.

Even faster, obviously, would be airlifts for those who need to cross a large number of states to access care—especially those reaching later gestations or with medical complications. The idea of privately flying patients may seem extreme, but it's not completely without precedent. Already there are groups like Air Care Alliance (http://www.aircarealliance.org/directory-groups) that organize volunteer pilots who have their own personal aircrafts and are willing to donate their time to transport people who require medical care. There is no reason not to believe there are pilots who would be happy to help abortion patients in need if someone just reached out to them.

Obviously vans, charter buses, hostels, airlifts, and the like are major expenses (and in some cases probably outright pipe dreams) and would require massive fund-raising and a large amount of coordination between local and national volunteers. But it is a network that has to exist in a post-*Roe* era, and it is our job to do everything we can to be sure that those already building this network have the resources they need to complete it.

Giving without Giving Yourself Away

Of course, there may be some people who want to give their support to these causes but are concerned about privacy. Maybe they are worried that a partner or family member will see a donation on a credit card statement or a canceled check, or they may have other reasons to try to keep their support as anonymous as possible, especially in hostile red states. For that reason I have tried to include physical addresses whenever possible so financial donations, gift cards, and other assistance can be sent directly to organizations. I have also included phone numbers for those without mailing addresses, with the hopes that potential donors who don't want to donate online can call directly to get an address if it is unlisted.

Chapter 5 Worksheet
Organizing an Anti-Anti-Abortion Protest

There should never be a protest at an abortion clinic—either by abortion opponents OR by abortion rights supporters. But maybe you really want a way to protest the protesters? Here are a few ideas to get you started, developed by activists with Abortion Access Force:

- *Pick your target:* Do you have a local crisis pregnancy center that has been known to lie to pregnant people about their services? Is there a church group that is always showing up at your local clinic? Is there a certain restaurant or other business that is known for supporting anti-abortion protests? Choose your place to protest carefully and consider a meaningful time to make your stand. The best counterprotests usually happen at anti-abortion events, so find one and get prepared.

- *Don't go alone:* No person should ever go protest a place by themselves—there is always safety in numbers. Maybe your partner doesn't want to protest with you, but at least be sure someone else is there to act as a witness in case there is some sort of escalation. If you can, gather a large group, and then designate one person to be outside the protest to handle any police, bystanders, or other issues that might arise.

- *Decide what kind of protest you want to make:* Are you going to drown out a speaker at an event? Are you going to stand silently? Will you be using signs or other props? Make sure you decide ahead of time what kind of protest you will be doing and be sure you have everything you need before you get there. Have your signs ready, or a bullhorn or noise-makers, wear clothing that will either make a statement or give you the most flexibility of movement. Signs that address specific anti-abortion activists who behave horribly at clinics are always in favor.

- *Bring a camera:* Many of the anti-abortion protesters wear cameras strapped to them to document any pos-sible issues or assaults. Others ask a partner to do the filming. Either way, you don't want to go without something to record the inter-action, just in case something happens and it's your word against whomever you are protesting.

- *Know the laws:* Are you on public or private ground? Are there rules against loitering? Do you need to keep moving or are you allowed to stand in one place? Will your body or signs obstruct the sidewalk? Could a sign handle be consid-ered a weapon? Research all the possible local ordinances (loitering laws, sound or amplification limits, occupancy rules), before you protest, so you are ready for any accusa-tions that may be made against you.

Let's Talk About Reproductive Justice

There is a common misconception that "reproductive rights" and "reproductive justice" are two synonyms that can be used interchangeably. They most definitely are not. The reproductive rights framework advocates and organizes on behalf of abortion and contraception rights. Reproductive justice, on the other hand, focuses on other equally important issues including reproductive health care access, pregnancy and childbirth, maternal mortality, reproductive technology and assistance, and so on. The framework intentionally includes these issues but also goes far beyond just reproductive health and rights to highlight the intersections of race, class, gender, socioeconomic status, immigration status, religion, and the other intersections of women and people's lives. Birthed by Black feminists and led by women and queer people of color, reproductive justice organizations center the voices of the marginalized, dismantling the racial and economic power structures that have kept middle- and upper-class white women in leadership roles and at the helm of activism campaigns. Reproductive justice focuses on an intersection of all human rights, while other frameworks offer a siloed, less effective strategy that does not center those most vulnerable. According to SisterSong, one of the leading reproductive justice organizations in the nation, "Abortion access is critical, and women of color and other marginalized women also often have difficulty accessing: contraception, comprehensive sex education, STI prevention and care, alternative birth options, adequate prenatal and pregnancy care, domestic violence assistance, adequate wages to support our families, safe homes, and so much more."[35]

While a lot of organizations may claim to support reproductive justice, there is little to show that they are living the tenets. Now, we not only have the opportunity to change that, but we have the obligation too. Less than 25 percent of Hispanic women and less than 4 percent of Black women voted for President Trump in the 2016 election, yet an astounding 52 percent of white women supported him—and pushed him into the White House.[36] Our current reproductive rights national leadership remains nearly as monolithic in race, age, and geography as they have been since *Roe* was decided nearly fifty years ago. Losing *Roe* gives us the perfect foundation to start again from scratch, rebuilding the movement as local, grassroots, intersectional, and focused on decentralizing power and resources and instead investing it with those who have been and will be the most affected by the policies.

The summer of 2020 brought an awakening for white allies to better understand their role moving forward during this period of racial, economic, and social upheaval. The murders of Breonna Taylor and George Floyd at the hands of local police lit the fire that turned into a national reckoning and a realization that unless each white person stands up and actively dismantles white supremacy in every action, justice will never occur.

We must deliberately and purposefully bring anti-racism into every action we take. That means centering Black, Indigenous, People of Color (BIPOC) in every level of activism, and stepping back our support of white-led organizations that ignore—or, even worse, outright appropriate—the cause of reproductive justice as their own.

Most of this handbook is filled with actions on how to give. This is the one chapter where instead we will discuss how to take. If we are ever going to build a truly intersectional movement concentrated on true social justice, we have to support and build up the groups that are already doing that work, but just as importantly we have to send a message to organizations and advocates that aren't willing to apply a reproductive justice lens to the work they do.

Before you consider donating, volunteering, or otherwise working with a national organization doing work around reproductive health or rights, ask yourself these questions.

Are there any people of color in leadership in this organization?

Have I looked at their board? Do they have diverse members from different communities on it?

Is there a reproductive justice group already working in this same area? Have I reached out to them first?

Has this organization formed a coalition with other groups that center marginalized communities in their activism and leadership? If so, are they actively allowing the other groups to lead?

Does this organization have a reputation for supporting the best practices of local organizers in a hands-off manner, instead of silencing local activists to fit the greater national message?

Does this organization have a reputation for supporting women of color rather than co-opting their work?

If you can't answer yes to each of these questions, simply don't donate or volunteer, and make it clear to them exactly why you won't. Make a pledge to refuse to work with any organization that doesn't prioritize marginalized leadership or voices or directly address racism and its effects on economic and social power structures. If every person vows to only support nonprofits and political groups that prioritize and elevate women and queer people of color, especially in their own communities and regions, reproductive health and rights groups will be forced to look at their own teams and campaigns and acknowledge the white privilege that has kept them in power even as the rights they claim to be dedicated to protecting eroded under their leadership.

Roe was a national decision that was immediately attacked on a state front by legislative restrictions, an attack that successfully stole abortion access from poor women and women of color years before the threat of *Roe* being overturned became a reality. We can no longer afford to keep taking a national approach to reproductive health and rights that continues to segregate political action and power from the communities that are the most impacted.

"National reproductive health and rights groups have created a culture of movement building placing us all on the defense, not the offense. Our work can no longer be reactive but must be strategic. Otherwise we will remain vulnerable as a conglomerate of movements and our various bases even more vulnerable," said Cherisse Scott, CEO and founder of SisterReach in Tennessee. "The real threat of losing *Roe* offers an opportunity for us to start again, and this time with women and queer people of color in every aspect of leadership, including in philanthropy, research, strategy, and movement building."

A list of reproductive justice groups follows, broken down by region. New groups are also being created every day, and SisterSong, SisterReach, New Voices for Reproductive Justice, and National Asian Pacific American Women's Forum (NAPAWF) are doing regionally based organizing and mobilization, which need sustained financial support to continue their important work.

Donating, volunteering, and otherwise supporting reproductive justice groups are the most impactful actions a person can take in a post-*Roe* America. These groups have been and continue to be the force doing much of the grassroots work in their communities, which have always been the hardest hit by restrictions.

National

Advocates for Youth

1325 G St. NW, Suite 980, Washington, DC 20005
202-419-3420
http://www.advocatesforyouth.org/
http://www.advocatesforyouth.org/about-us/contact

Black Mamas Matter Alliance

1237 Ralph David Abernathy Blvd., Atlanta, GA 30310
https://blackmamasmatter.org/
info@blackmamasmatter.org

Black Women's Health Imperative

55 M St. SE, Suite 940, Washington, DC 20003
202-787-5931
https://www.bwhi.org/
info@bwhi.org

In Our Own Voice/National Black Women's Reproductive Justice Agenda

1012 14th St. NW, Suite 450, Washington, DC 20005
202-545-7660
http://blackrj.org/

Interfaith Voices for Reproductive Justice

http://iv4rj.org/
https://www.facebook.com/IV4RJ/
interfaith4rj@gmail.com

National Asian Pacific American Women's Forum (NAPAWF)

773-251-8440
https://www.napawf.org/
info@napawf.org

National Latina Institute for Reproductive Health

212-422-2553
http://latinainstitute.org/en
http://latinainstitute.org/es
HumanResources@latinainstitute.org

Native American Women's Health Education Resource Center

PO Box 572, Lake Andes, SD 57356-0572
605-487-7072
http://www.nativeshop.org/

SisterSong

1237 Ralph David Abernathy Blvd., Atlanta, GA 30310
404-756-2680
https://www.sistersong.net/
info@sistersong.net

Women Engaged

https://www.womenengaged.org/
info@womenengaged.org

Western/Mountain

Colorado Doula Project

https://www.coloradodoulaproject.com/

Colorado Organization for Latina Opportunity and Reproductive Rights (COLOR)

PO Box 40991, Denver, CO 80204
303-393-0382
https://www.colorlatina.org/
info@colorlatina.org

Indigenous Women Rising

505-398-1990
https://www.iwrising.org/
indigenouswomenrising@gmail.com

Young Women United

309 Gold St. SW, Albuquerque, NM 87102
505-831-8930

201 N. Church, Suite 320, Las Cruces, NM 88001
575-526-7964

https://youngwomenunited.org

Strong Families New Mexico/Forward Together

400 Gold Ave. SW, Suite 900, Albuquerque, NM 87102
505-842-8070
https://forwardtogether.org/
info@forwardtogether.org

Forward Together

300 Frank H. Ogawa Plaza, Suite 700, Oakland, CA 94612
510-663-8300

5020 NE Martin Luther King Jr. Blvd., Portland, OR 97214
510-663-8300, ext. 348

https://forwardtogether.org/
info@forwardtogether.org

Black Women for Wellness

PO Box 292516, Los Angeles, CA 90029
323-290-5955
http://www.bwwla.org
info@bwwla.com

California Latinas for Reproductive Justice

PO Box 861766, Los Angeles, CA 90086
213-270-5258
https://californialatinas.org/
info@clrj.org

Southern

SPARK Reproductive Justice Now

PO Box 89210, Atlanta, GA 30312
404-331-3250
http://www.sparkrj.org/
info@sparkrj.org

SisterLove

PO Box 10558, Atlanta, GA 30310-1731
404-505-7777
https://www.sisterlove.org/
info@sisterlove.org

Lift Louisiana

PO Box 792063, New Orleans, LA 70179
504-484-9636
http://liftlouisiana.org/

Women with a Vision

1226 N. Broad St., New Orleans, LA 70119
504-301-0428
http://wwav-no.org/

SisterReach

2725 Kirby Rd., Suite 15, Memphis, TN 38119
901-614-9906
http://sisterreach.org

BirthStrides

Memphis, TN
https://www.birthstrides.org/
https://www.birthstrides.org/contact.html

Afiya Center

Dallas, TX
972-629-9266
https://theafiyacenter.org/
info@theafiyacenter.org

South Texans for Reproductive Justice

https://www.facebook.com/SoTX4ReproJustice/
sotx4rj@gmail.com

Yellowhammer Fund

Tuscaloosa, AL
205-582-4950
https://yellowhammerfund.org
info@yellowhammerfund.org

Eastern/Midwest

Illinois Caucus for Adolescent Health

719 S. State St., Floor 4, Chicago, IL 60605
312-427-4460
https://www.icah.org
info@icah.org

New Voices for Reproductive Justice

New Voices Pittsburgh, 5987 Broad St., Pittsburgh, PA 15206
412-363-4500
http://www.newvoicespittsburgh.org/
info@newvoicespittsburgh.org

New Voices Cleveland

2200 Fairhill Rd., Cleveland, OH 44120
412-363-4500
info@newvoicespittsburgh.org

New Voices Philadelphia

3853 Lancaster Ave., Philadelphia, PA 19104
412-363-4500
info@newvoicespittsburgh.org

Restoring Our Own Through Transformation (ROOTT)

Columbus, OH
614-398-1766
https://www.roott.org/

IndyFeminists

https://www.facebook.com/IndyFems

Chapter 6 Worksheet

Is Your Activism Steeped in White Supremacy? (A Checklist)

1) *Are you listening to BIPOC voices or speaking over them?*
   Being an ally means centering those who are being harmed. If

you are a white person speaking, pass the microphone. If you are being offered a platform—speaking, writing, organizing—consider suggesting a BIPOC candidate who can take your place, and provide their contact information to make the transition easy. If a person of color tells you your activism is hurting them or the movement, listen and process, don't argue. Even hold your apologies until later, in order to avoid centering the conversation back on you. Remember that you have been conditioned by a society that marginalizes BIPOC voices. Learning is part of the deconditioning process, so don't take offense, take advice.

2) *Are you being performative?*

"Naked Athena," the nude white woman who yoga'd her way into the headlines in July 2020 during the Portal occupation, didn't halt any riots or protect anyone from being kettled or teargassed by federal agents. Instead, she turned the conversation away from the #Blacklivesmatter activists who were raising awareness of police brutality and racial injustice in their city. Was "Athena" drawing awareness to her white privilege, or derailing the work of Black activists under attack? Was she aware of what she was doing or simply taking advantage of a moment? What was her message, and was it in line with the BLM movement? And was she taking up or diverting resources that could have been better used to support the protests themselves? Know what your activism is doing and how it may detrimentally impact those who are truly doing the work. Acknowledge the fact that it is your own white privilege that allows you the opportunity to be performative in the first place, without the fear of being policed for it.

3) *Are you demanding education?*

No one owes you their time; the responsibility is on you to grow your own awareness and knowledge. Don't understand a term? Confused about why certain actions are being condemned and not others? Don't expect BIPOC activists to get you up to speed. Do your own research, find your own sources. Your allyship shouldn't cause the people you are organizing with to do even more work. Also, remember that not all experiences, terminology, oppressions, or types of education are universal for all people of color. Your Latinx comrade will have different experiences than your Black friend. If a BIPOC activist says something you believe is harmful, it is not your place as a white person to call out a person of color over how to organize their own community. If what the person said is truly harmful, you can be sure that another community member will address it themselves.

4) *Are you using your privilege to cause harm rather than help?*
Follow the lead of POC and do not under any circumstances escalate a situation. "A white person's job at a protest isn't to spray-paint 'Black Lives Matter' on a building," Black activist Ben O'Keefe told Vox.com.[37] "It's not to destroy stuff. It's not to loot stores. Their job is not to mess with the cops and throw stuff. Their job at that protest, what they are there to do, is to do everything they can in their power to put their bodies between the bodies of Black people and police . . . Because not only is it disrespectful to disrupt our protests, but it actually is also doing direct harm to the Black lives that these folks are supposed to be there to try to protect." This is especially true when it comes to any form of violence. Do NOT come to a protest with the intention of getting hurt—it is not a badge of honor, and it increases the danger for everyone.

5) *Are you taking resources from the groups already doing the work?*
If you want to start an action—be it a march, a volunteer orga-

nization, or a political campaign—be aware of who is already in the space. Support those who are already on the ground rather than building something new—and give more than a cursory glance to see if you are replicating anyone else's efforts. If you can't be bothered to fully research the landscape, you probably shouldn't be launching an action in the first place.

6) *Are you using POC as shields?*

Having a handful of BIPOC participants doesn't inoculate you from benefiting from white supremacy—especially if all of the power still remains centered in white leadership. It's not enough to work with people of color, you must be working both for and under. Diversity should be evident in every layer of the organization—not just in its photo ops.

7) *Is your advocacy embedded in your daily actions too?*

If you are organizing a rally to say that #Blacklivesmatter but refusing to provide a bottle of water to a Black man walking past your table at the event, your advocacy is performative. If you are claiming to work intersectionally but your employees are paid less depending on race or gender presentation, you are steeped in white supremacy. It's not enough to uplift BIPOC voices when you are looking for vendors and speakers if you aren't applying the same diligence in your day-to-day interactions too.

Knowing Your Comfort Zone

Why Civil Disobedience?

Access to abortion and birth control isn't just a health care issue or an economic issue, it's also a civil rights issue, and like every civil rights battle, gains are often made through acts of civil disobedience, or working outside the legal framework. Married people officially gained the right to access birth control only after Estelle Griswold, the executive director of the Planned Parenthood League of Connecticut, opened a clinic and began offering contraception in direct opposition to the 1960s state law forbidding it. That right was extended to single people in 1972 after Bill Baird was arrested in 1967 for purposely flaunting the Massachusetts law and publicly providing contraceptives to an unmarried woman during a college lecture. The Clergy Consultation Service on Abortion spent much of the 1960s and early '70s prior to the *Roe* decision assisting pregnant people in finding safe abortions either from legal or illegal providers throughout the country and across the borders, and there were groups like Jane's Collective that provided the service themselves even at the risk of their own arrest.

Today people are highlighting a number of issues through acts of civil disobedience. North Carolina had weekly mass arrests at their state capitol during Moral Mondays protests, while the Black Lives Matter movement physically closed highways with their bodies. When Brett

Kavanaugh was appointed to the Supreme Court hundreds of activists were arrested—some multiple times—for interrupting his hearing, protesting in the Hart Building when it became clear the Senate Judiciary was not going to investigate charges of past sexual assault—some protestors even blocked the stairs prior to Kavanaugh's swearing-in ceremony.[38] Now we are seeing public protest as a daily occurrence, from the weeks of protest after the murder of George Floyd by Minneapolis police officers to the occupation of Portland, Chicago, and other major cities by federal troops claiming to be subduing dangerous (and of course mostly progressive) cities. As our society recedes further into racism, sexism, xenophobia, and classism, opposing the power structure through nonviolent means grows more imperative.

That is why we should be thinking now about how we will defy the government in the event that *Roe v. Wade* is overturned and states are allowed to fully ban abortion.

"If *Roe* is overturned or gutted, it is certain that some states will propose and enact new abortion bans. Again, nonviolent civil disobedience should remain on the table, this time targeting state and municipal-level lawmakers," writes Erin Matson, the cofounder of the reproductive rights group ReproAction, in *Teen Vogue*.[39] "We must remember that while in several contexts abortion rights supporters lack immediate political power—in spite of the fact that nearly seven in ten Americans do not want to see *Roe* overturned—we always retain the power of using our bodies to slow or stop the machinery of state repression."

Matson adds, "Ultimately, it is up to activists to decide—are we willing to break convention if lobbying fails? Are we willing to strategically expose ourselves to the risk of arrest? And if we are not, are we willing to look into the eyes of the future generations who will be incarcerated for abortions, miscarriages, and pregnancy complications?'"

ReproAction is a growing network of state-based activists that conducts political events, teach-ins, and other direct actions to increase access to abortion and birth control services. They currently have national campaigns as well as individual campaigns in DC, Virginia, Missouri, Arkansas, and Wisconsin. You can join up with or financially support ReproAction to increase their national and local reach.

ReproAction

https://reproaction.org/
https://reproaction.org/contact-us/
https://donatenow.networkforgood.org/reproaction

Is Civil Disobedience Right for Me?

What are you willing to do to make sure you, the people you know, or even total strangers have access to contraception and abortion care—especially once more abortion options become illegal? Are you willing to be arrested if you participate in direct action or non-violent protest? Is helping someone obtain abortion pills worth a potential prison sentence? Would you drive a teen to another state to get an abortion if that drive makes you an abortion "facilitator" and a federal criminal?

These are all questions that need to be considered now that both state and federal governments have announced their willingness to prosecute anyone who even assists with an illegal abortion in the future.

In the spring of 2019, the Georgia state legislature passed a ban on all abortions at the point when embryonic heart tones can be detected—about six weeks' gestation or two weeks after a missed period. As part of the ban (which as of August 2020 is still blocked from being enacted), a "person" was legally redefined as the results of a pregnancy any point after the fertilization of an egg. The fallout, according to Mark Joseph Stern of Slate, is that should the bill ever actually be allowed to take effect, any act of assisting a pregnant person to obtain an abortion could be viewed as a felony.

"If a Georgia resident plans to travel elsewhere to obtain an abortion, she may be charged with conspiracy to commit murder, punishable by 10 years' imprisonment," Stern wrote. "An individual who helps a woman plan her trip to get an out-of-state abortion, or transports her to the clinic, may also be charged with conspiracy. These individuals, after all, are 'conspiring' to end the life of a 'person' with 'full legal recognition' under Georgia law."[40]

You may believe you are willing to risk everything to help someone get an abortion—and that may very well be what is needed in some cases in a post-*Roe* America. But make sure that you've really thought out all of the consequences of such a radical approach.

These are the questions you should be asking yourself now, before the laws are put in place.

Am I the Only One Who Can Help?

One small silver lining of Trump's time in office is the way it energized so many people to actively resist the political agenda. There are more activists, donors, candidates, and protesters than there have been in decades, and that means lots of people who can work together and step in when and where people are needed.

But in certain geographic areas it is and will continue to be harder to find those with the ability and privilege to do resistance work. For example, the increased militarization of ICE and border security means checkpoints into and out of America will be more scrutinized than ever before. With a population that in many cases is literally trapped in places like the Rio Grande Valley or Las Cruces, where undocumented people can neither leave the country for services nor go further into the US for care, the need for additional action (and people who have the willingness and ability to act) may be much greater than in New York City or the Bay Area.

Maybe you have a very specific skill set. You might be medically trained, have a legal background, or maybe you've done counseling or social work or you are a member of the clergy. These are people who will add a lot of value to the movement, especially if it turns out civil disobedience is the way to proceed.

Ask yourself if you are the only person who can do the thing you are considering doing, or if there are a number of people like you who are planning to step up. Then ask yourself what sort of risk you may be running and see how those factors balance out.

Do I Like to Work Alone or with Groups?

It's almost impossible to be a solitary activist these days, but there are spaces where you can manage. Letter-writing campaigns, social media campaigns, information distribution, and fund-raising can all be accomplished in a fairly solitary environment. But realize you will still need to work with other people in some form—they are unavoidable. If you are comfortable with one-on-one interaction and just don't enjoy group settings, a practical support action (driving patients, lending out a space for them to stay, etc.) or Plan B distribution might be a good way to balance the two.

If you are a person who thrives in a group setting, consider activities like clinic escorting, protesting (in appropriate venues), lobbying at the capital, or other forms of abortion action trainings.

Is My Privacy Important?

If we get to a point where abortion is mostly or completely illegal, that means we are also at a point where if you do offer any sort of assistance, you can expect to be targeted by those who oppose abortion. This will happen regardless of whether your activism is legal or not, and it is already happening to those who support abortion patients and clinics.

Are you ready to have abortion opponents looking for your name or your address? Would you be okay with photos or videos of you being shared on social media, either with or without your name attached? Are you worried about losing your job if your employer gets ID'ed and harassed? Will you be uncomfortable if people mention the names of your children or in some other way show that they know about your personal life as a means of trying to intimidate you?

These are not hypotheticals. Each and every one of these examples are commonplace for abortion providers, clinic owners, clinic escorts, even some well-known abortion rights activists. And if *Roe* is overturned, the attacks will only intensify.

Am I Worried About My Family?

Do you need to be concerned about your family's physical safety if you become completely invested in abortion access when *Roe* is overturned? Hopefully not. However, there is a lot more to protecting your family than just ensuring their physical safety. In the '80s–'90s Rescue Movement days, providers and others associated with clinics reported their own children being verbally harassed by strangers and in some cases even followed by anti-abortion activists when they were in public, such as at their schools. More recently, abortion opponents picketed a clinic landlord's children's elementary school to try to get him to stop renting to one provider (that landlord eventually sold the building after years of constant harassment).

Privacy can never be completely guaranteed, and you simply have to prepare yourself for the absolute worst-case scenario. If you are worried about how your children or other family members might be targeted because of your actions, the best decision is to find a different way to be involved.

What Would Happen if I Were in Jail?

Is your family dependent upon you financially? Are you the caretaker either for children or for other relatives? Would you lose a job or relationship if you were imprisoned for any length of time? Would it be impossible for you to find a new job, or rent or buy a home with a possible criminal charge on your record? Are you willing to lose your ability to vote if that charge ends up being a felony? Could it be used against you in a custody situation? Is there someone else who can pay your bills or feed your pets?

Some of these questions may seem serious, others far-fetched. But they all need to be considered before you decide how much you are willing to give up when it comes to civil disobedience. An arrest for a peaceful demonstration would still impact your life in ways you may not have considered. An arrest for something far more serious, like being an accessory to an illegal abortion, is something else. For communities of color, the likelihood and severity of punishment is increased regardless of the peacefulness of the action due to the internal racial bias of our police and judicial system. It may be even more dangerous for those who are accused of helping someone procure an illegal abortion, since the groundwork for jailing "accomplices" is already in place.

In Pennsylvania, one mother was given a sentence of up to eighteen months in prison for giving her daughter misoprostol to end her pregnancy when the two were unable to find an affordable nearby clinic to use. This happened while abortion was still legal in that state. Imagine what the consequences may be once abortion is made illegal—and consider them all carefully before you act.[41]

Would My Partner and Family Support Me?

Once you have finished asking yourself all of these questions, go back and ask them of the people you live with. If your partner/parent/roommate/etc. is unable to support you in your actions, definitely rethink your plans. Getting more aggressively involved in abortion access while laws are being overturned has the potential to be emotionally and financially exhausting, and if you do not have a support network (either because they don't support your activism on an emotional level or because they believe they are unable to take up your responsibilities if necessary), you need to know that and come up with alternative ways to take action.

Above all else, if you do not feel comfortable enough with your partner or family to even ask these questions, that means you should consider a different way to support patients seeking abortion care.

Do I Fit the "Profile"?

Unsurprisingly, the best people to commit acts of civil disobedience or conscientious lawbreaking are often white. Because communities of color are already in many cases living under a police state and are bearing the greatest burden of the racist enforcement of current laws, civil disobedience is one of the biggest places where white allies can step in and have the most impact politically.

been arrested and other personal details, so consider speaking with a professional ahead of time about likely costs.

5) *Bring your ID—and keep it on your body.*

Your bags will be taken from you. Make sure that you have ID on you, and also that it is somewhere physically accessible to you, like inside your pocket, a bra cup, or a sock.

6) *But try to leave everything else at home.*

You will be searched, and you could lose your belongings. Try to carry as little with you as possible in order to mitigate any lost or destroyed items.

7) *Lock your phone.*

If you bring your phone with you, make sure that it is locked, and that it cannot be opened with facial recognition or your fingerprint. Set it to only open for a PIN, and reset that again once you are released.

What to Know About Self-Managed Abortion Care with Abortion Pills and/or Herbs

Two days after President Donald Trump's inauguration, an editor from the United Kingdom approached me with an assignment—reporting on the likelihood of DIY (self-induced, "do-it-yourself") abortion taking over the country now that the federal government was under Republican control. It didn't take me long to learn that it was a topic at the front of everyone's mind. In April 2017 Women Help Women announced the launch of an online support service called Self-Managed Abortion: Safe and Supported (SASS) to offer information and counseling to those trying to end their pregnancies through abortion-inducing medications outside a clinical setting. As SASS's US spokesperson Susan Yanow told the *Guardian*, "People are not being advised to use the pills. They're being advised if they've already decided to use the pills. What drives this project is the knowledge that women have been managing this on their own."[46]

Those who want to end a pregnancy but either can't access a clinic or prefer to manage their own abortions have been using herbs and abortion pills since long before Trump's surprise electoral win. Herbal abortions have existed for as long as there have been midwives, medicine women, and pregnancy. Today's herbal abortion attempts are often far less effective due to misleading or incorrect information on the Internet and no medically vetted, detailed directions on how to use herbs correctly that the general public can easily access. Herbs also tend to require action as early as possible in the pregnancy and are a long-term commitment since they take time to work.

Using medication (mifepristone plus misoprostol or misoprostol alone) to effectively induce a miscarriage, however, is a much more recent (and effective) option. Mifepristone (RU-486) was approved by the FDA for use in the US in 2000 and offered as a medication-only option for terminating a pregnancy outside an abortion clinic. As part of a protocol developed first by the FDA and later streamlined by medical professionals through their own clinical use and more than a decade of research, patients were now able to obtain medicine in the clinic and take the dose of mifepristone there, then take miso-prostol home to finish the termination in private. Current research shows that medication abortion can and is being used to easily and safely end pregnancies independent of a clinic and with minimal risk to a patient—at least, minimal medical risk. The biggest health risk for self-managed abortion care using abortion pills is that those who attempt to induce their own abortions may not seek out medical assis-tance in the rare case that there is a complication, fearing a doctor or hospital may then report them to law enforcement.

Again, to be clear, multiple studies from mainstream medical journals state that medication abortion conducted independent of a provider is a safe and effective means of ending a pregnancy—as long as the person terminating is not forced to hide their actions out of fear of legal punishment. It is the criminal code—not the medica-tions themselves—that makes self-managed abortion care risky.

The following sections are reprints of information found on the Internet or taken from medical sources, and are simply a compila-tion of what information has been published regarding herbal and medication abortions in a nonclinical setting. This is not meant to encourage any decisions regarding abortion care. In many states in the US it is illegal to purchase medications online from outside the country, and in some states it is illegal to purposely terminate a pregnancy if you are not a medical provider or if you are doing it outside a hospital or clinic. However, it is not illegal to research or to share scientific and medical information, especially when that information is about health care that may affect more than half of the population.

This is only information, and not legal or medical advice. If a person were seeking information about self-managing an abortion using medications and herbs, this is the type of information that they would find by searching the Internet.

Herbal Abortion

It isn't easy to find information online about inducing miscarriage with herbs, and googling brings up a lot of nonspecific information ("ingest a lot of Vitamin C" or "insert parsley into your vagina"). Sometimes that information conflicts with other sources and some instructions can be potentially dangerous. According to those with experience in herbal abortions, there are a lot of misconceptions on the Internet, especially when it comes to how and when herbs should be used.

In general best practices, using herbs to try to induce a miscarriage must be done as soon as a person believes they may be pregnant in order to have any potential success, and even then there is no guarantee that it will work. According to Sister Zeus, the reference point for most of the at-home herbal abortion information on the Internet (but again, not a medically vetted or endorsed site), if an abortion hasn't been successful by about six weeks (two weeks after the period should have arrived), it's unlikely it will work at all.[47]

By sorting through multiple websites one does find a few commonalities, usually involving the use of parsley. One site suggests that as soon as a person realizes their period is late, that person should insert fresh parsley into the vagina, removing and replacing it with new sprigs every twelve hours, while also taking a tincture of between two and six tablespoons of a parsley infusion every four hours (a tincture should be made by adding one ounce parsley stems to two and a half cups of boiling water, removing the water from the heat, and then allowing the mixture to steep for one to two hours). In addition, a person should also ingest five hundred milligrams of vitamin C every hour, maxing out at six thousand milligrams a day.

As you can see, even these instructions are still frustratingly imprecise, and the results are only partially guaranteed, which is why so few people manage to successfully induce miscarriages using herbs. Even more alarming is the assumption that just because something is "herbal" rather than medication based, it can't harm you.

In Argentina, where an August 2018 attempt to legalize abortion in the first trimester failed to pass the senate, a woman died just days after attempting to induce her own miscarriage using herbs. According to reports, the thirty-four-year-old woman named Elizabeth already had a two-year-old and, unable to obtain an abortion in Argentina, attempted to induce labor by inserting parsley into her vagina. When an infection developed, she was afraid to go to a hospital out of fear of jail for attempting her own abortion, waiting until she developed sepsis before seeking care. Her uterus was removed, but she died anyway, another victim of the country's abortion ban.[48]

Remember—herbal doesn't automatically mean safe, either in miscarriage induction or in any other setting. But there are midwives, herbalists, and traditional healers who have developed processes that can be effective if done early and correctly. The following slides are provided by Emily Likins-Ehlers of Revolutionary Motherhood (Twitter handle @revolutionary_motherhood), who has streamlined herbal miscarriage induction information developed from Sage-Femme Collective's 2008 book *Natural Liberty: Re-dis-covering Self-Induced Abortion Methods.* These herbal methods are believed to be the safest recipes that can be made from easily available supplies, and the least likely to be fatally toxic. If a person does choose to follow these instructions as a means of self-inducing, they must pay very close attention to warning signs of infection or toxicity. Remember that these instructions are not provided by a medical doctor and should not be considered medical advice, but are only for information-sharing purposes.

HERBAL
ABORTION
© @REVOLUTIONARY_MOTHERHOOD

effective in the first trimester, most
effective before your missed period

FROM: "NATURAL LIBERTY"
BY THE SAGE-FEMME COLLECTIVE

disclaimer:
i'm not a doctor.
this is ancient wisdom and nothing is guaranteed.
practice good sense.

AVOCADO
SEED
@REVOLUTIONARY_MOTHERHOOD

INSTRUCTIONS:
grate an entire avocado seed (pit) into 1 cup of water & allow to steep overnight. strain liquid. drink 2-3 oz of liquid every three to four hours until bleeding begins.

SWIPE FOR WARNINGS & CONTRADITIONS TO CARE

AVOCADO
SEED
@REVOLUTIONARY_MOTHERHOOD

PLEASE READ:
*****WARNINGS AND CONTRADICTION TO CARE*****

avocado seed drink can trigger allergies to latex and banana

avocado seed toxicity can lead to lung congestion, mastitis, tissue edema, milk reduction, and death

discontinue if you have signs of toxicity specific to Avocado:

gastro-intenstial irritation, vomiting, diarrhea, respiratory distress, congestion, or fluid accumulation in feet or face.

CASTOR OIL
@REVOLUTIONARY_MOTHERHOOD

INSTRUCTIONS:
cold-pressed castor oil can be found in many stores. it can be combined with ginger and grated papaya seeds for increased effectiveness. take 2 oz. of castor oil with 12 oz. lukewarm milk. repeat in 2 hours if bleed has not yet begun.

SWIPE FOR WARNINGS & CONTRADITIONS TO CARE

CASTOR OIL
@REVOLUTIONARY_MOTHERHOOD

PLEASE READ:
*****WARNINGS AND CONTRADICTION TO CARE*****

castor oil should not be used by people who have urinary tract or gastro-intestinal infections.

castor oil will cause diarrhea, and can cause vomiting, dehydration, and in rare cases, gastrointestinal bleeding.

discontinue if you have signs of toxicity specific to castor oil:

clammy skin, chills, reduced pulse, violent vomiting.

CHAMOMILE
@REVOLUTIONARY_MOTHERHOOD

INSTRUCTIONS:

five drops chamomile essential oil in yoni steam or sitz bath. combine with ginger for more effectiveness.
DO NOT BOIL CHAMOMILE.
for more info visit *steamychick.com/diy/*

SWIPE FOR WARNINGS & CONTRADITIONS TO CARE

CHAMOMILE
@REVOLUTIONARY_MOTHERHOOD

PLEASE READ:
*****WARNINGS AND CONTRADICTION TO CARE*****

chamomile has a calming effect.

if you are allergic to ragweed, aster, or chrysanthemum--take caution

discontinue if you have signs of toxicity specific to chamomile:

nausea, vomiting, vertigo, personality changes, delirium, and hallucinations

GARLIC

@REVOLUTIONARY_MOTHERHOOD

INSTRUCTIONS:

simmer a garlic bulb in water for ten minutes. it can be combined with parsley for increased effectiveness. test the temperature of the water, and then douche with the garlic water.

when cool, place the simmered garlic bulb in a cheesecloth and insert into the vagina. replace every 10 hours for up to six days.

discontinue use if discomfort or irritation occurs.

ONION

@REVOLUTIONARY_MOTHERHOOD

INSTRUCTIONS:

Pessary: bake onion at 350 degrees F for one hour. cool & wrap in cheesecloth, tied with string, and inserted vaginally. replace every 8 hours and wear for up to 6 days.

OR

slice 4 onions with skins; boil for ten minutes in 1 quart of water. filter and sip throughout the day. can also be used for vaginal fumigation

discontinue use if negative side effects are experienced.

PAPAYA - LATEX

@REVOLUTIONARY_MOTHERHOOD

INSTRUCTIONS:

wash one unripe papaya fruit. using a sharp knife, make shallow scratches on the thin fruit skin. the Papaya Latex will ooze and run out of the cuts. Collect the latex.

Using a clean paintbrush and speculum, brush the papaya latex onto the cervical os

or, fill the vagina with papaya latex using a children's medicine syringe.

SWIPE FOR WARNINGS & CONTRADICTIONS TO CARE

HIBISCUS

@REVOLUTIONARY_MOTHERHOOD

INSTRUCTIONS:

add 1 cup fresh flowers or 10-16 Tbs. of dried flowers to to 2 pints hot water. can be prepared with papaya seeds or ginger to increase effectiveness.

Sip throughout the day, for up to 10 days

hibiscus rosa-sinensis
hibiscus phoenicia
hibiscus esculentus

discontinue use if negative side effects are experienced.

PAPAYA - SEEDS

@REVOLUTIONARY_MOTHERHOOD

INSTRUCTIONS:

eat 1-2 tbs. fresh papaya seeds taken two or three times a day for up to six days

SWIPE FOR WARNINGS & CONTRADICTIONS TO CARE

PAPAYA

@REVOLUTIONARY_MOTHERHOOD

PLEASE READ:
WARNINGS & CONTRADICTIONS TO CARE

Papaya latex is an irritant and some people are allergic to it. people with a known latex allergy should not use papaya.

Papaya fruit is green when unripe when orange when ripe. shopkeepers sometimes do not display unripe papaya, but will have them in storage.

Papaya seeds can cause gastro-intestinal distress. **Seek medical attention if symptoms become unmanageable.**

PARSLEY
@REVOLUTIONARY_MOTHERHOOD

INSTRUCTIONS:

Clean and chop one bunch of fresh curled, Italian or flat leaf parsley. Boil one quart of water and pour over herb - steep 30 minutes. Drink throughout the day for up to seven days.

Insert a few fresh parsley sprigs vaginally and replace every 12 hours.

**SWIPE FOR WARNINGS &
CONTRADICTIONS TO CARE**

PARSLEY
@REVOLUTIONARY_MOTHERHOOD

**PLEASE READ:
*WARNINGS & CONTRADICTIONS TO CARE***

▪ Parsley should not be used by individuals with inflammatory kidney disorders

▪ Parsley oil and tincture should be used with caution, as too much can cause hallucinations, paralysis, and liver and kidney degeneration.

Discontinue use if you have signs of toxicity specific to parsley:

Nausea, hallucinations, vomiting, vertigo, hives, photosensitivity, painful urination, dark-colored urine, or tremors.

PINEAPPLE
@REVOLUTIONARY_MOTHERHOOD

INSTRUCTIONS:

Upon waking, eat one whole pineapple. Unripe pineapple is most effective, and can be eaten with honey to make it more palatable. Unripe pineapple is green inside.

**SWIPE FOR WARNINGS &
CONTRADICTIONS TO CARE**

PINEAPPLE
@REVOLUTIONARY_MOTHERHOOD

**PLEASE READ:
*WARNINGS & CONTRADICTIONS TO CARE***

Do not use pineapple medicinally if you have a known allergy to pineapple.

Unripe pineapple is considered mostly inedible, and it can irritate the mouth and throat.

Pineapple in large amounts is likely to cause diarrhea - take care to stay hydrated

Discontinue use if you experience an increased heart rate or signs of an allergic reaction such as swelling, hives, or tightness in your chest or throat.

POMEGRANATE
@REVOLUTIONARY_MOTHERHOOD

INSTRUCTIONS:

Grind the inside of fresh pomegranate peel and seeds into water and apply to the cervix by inserting vaginally. A tied cheesecloth, a menstrual cup, or douching with the material may be effective methods.

**SWIPE FOR WARNINGS &
CONTRADICTIONS TO CARE**

POMEGRANATE
@REVOLUTIONARY_MOTHERHOOD

**PLEASE READ:
*WARNINGS & CONTRADICTIONS TO CARE***

Wash your hands before and after inserting anything into the vagina, and any tools that are inserted into the vagina should be washed with soap and water or can be boiled to disinfect.

discontinue use if vision becomes blurred or you experience prolonged dilation of pupils.

during COVID-19, or any other time, emergency medical care for miscarriage should only be sought if you are extremely ill, or if your symptoms become un-manageable.

you may use one full maxi pad quickly, or it may take hours. gushing is normal.

seek medical attention if:
- your gushing is prolonged.
- discharge is foul-smelling.
- your skin becomes pale and clammy.
- you develop a fever or core body temperature below 94 degrees F

Shepherd's purse (*Capsella bursa-pastoris*) tincture is often kept on-hand during home birth to help stop postpartum bleeding.

yoga, progressive relaxation, meditation, movement, & heating pads can help with discomfort.

utilize over-the-counter pain medication that you are familiar with.

don't hesitate to reach out to Emily @Revolutionary_Motherhood for support.

Medication Abortion

Unlike herbal abortion methods, which can be unreliable, long, labor intensive, and potentially ineffective or dangerous, medication abortion has been extensively studied through traditional medical channels. Misoprostol alone is effective in ending a pregnancy before twelve weeks 80 to 85 percent of the time. Mifepristone plus misoprostol is effective in ending a pregnancy before ten weeks 95 to 98 percent of the time.

Medication abortion as it is conducted in a clinic is actually a combination of the two medications—two hundred milligrams of mifepristone and eight hundred micrograms of misoprostol. Mifepristone will reduce the progesterone in a person's body by blocking progesterone receptors, ending the pregnancy. Misoprostol causes contractions, expelling from the womb the products of conception. Misoprostol is taken after the mifepristone, with the time interval depending on whether people place the tablets vaginally or buccally (between the cheek and gums).

People have also learned that miscarriage can be induced by using Misoprostol alone, although that is a bit less effective than the combination of the two medications. Those who research abortion-inducing medications often find that accessing misoprostol is easier than locating mifepristone and using the two medications together.

Where People Find Medications

Obviously, the most reliable place to find medication abortion is at an abortion clinic. Most clinics are able to provide mifepristone and misoprostol to their patients, and in some states patients are now able to obtain these medicines without even needing to go to the clinic. If you are seeking an abortion and live in Colorado, Georgia, Hawaii, Illinois, Iowa, Maine, Maryland, Minnesota, Montana, New Mexico, New York, Oregon, Washington, DC, or Washington State, you can visit www.telabortion.net and see if you qualify to receive medication by mail, and whether you will need a pre-screening ultrasound. In some cases, you may be able to get medications without leaving your home at all—especially if there are extenuating health care factors, such as the COVID-19 pandemic.

How Federal Agencies Have Blocked Abortion Access

Although medication abortion is quite safe medically, one of its medications—mifepristone—is still considered "high risk" by the FDA. When the drug was introduced on the market in the United States in 2000, the agency put it under Risk Evaluation and Mitigation Strategy (REMS) restrictions, and despite two decades of studies that have repeatedly shown a very low likelihood of adverse side effects, politics has kept REMS in place. That makes it impossible for individual doctors to prescribe it unless they are willing to provide extensive additional support. Most pharmacies are forbidden from stocking it, and until recently it was unable to be delivered through the mail. Some states removed these barriers on their own, but until recently, the majority still follow the federal guidelines, especially conservative states that do not want to allow any abortion at all.

But in a rare instance of abortion access expansion, a federal judge ruled in July 2020 that in order to limit possible exposure to COVID-19 the REMS protocol could be suspended,[49] and clinics and doctors would be able to mail medication directly to patients rather than only in face to face meetings. The Trump appointed FDA sued to block the suspension, but the Supreme Court allowed it to stay in place. That change opened up most states in the nation—as long as they did not have other restrictions such as telemedicine bans in place—to finally provide abortion pills by mail, making them more accessible physically (if not financially) for many pregnant people. At least for now.

However, many people are unable to access a clinic because of financial, logistical, or health issues, and those pregnant people are likely to look online in order to find websites where they can either purchase misoprostol or mifepristone plus misoprostol in a "combipack," or find information on where to purchase those medicines. PlanCPills.org is a website that provides information on medication abortion options for those unable to access an abortion clinic. If a person were to click on "Information about abortion pills" and then the question "How can I find abortion pills?" they would learn the following:

- That abortion in the first twelve weeks of pregnancy can be done safely using misoprostol alone (80 to 85 percent effective) or mifepristone plus misoprostol (95 to 98 percent effective). Abortion pills cause a miscarriage if used correctly.
- Misoprostol is available in pharmacies, with a prescription. Misoprostol is used to prevent ulcers in people with conditions like arthritis that require them to take nonsteroidal anti-inflammatory (NSAID) medication long-term.
- Misoprostol is available from some Internet veterinary supply stores and veterinarians, as it is used to treat ulcers and arthritis in dogs.
- Misoprostol is available over the counter in many Latin American countries.
- Online pharmacies in Canada sell misoprostol inexpensively,

and it has been reported that some may not require a pre-scription.

- Combination packs of mifepristone and misoprostol together are also available on the Internet.

Prior to 2020, Plan C also offered a selection of websites through which a person could purchase medications, scored based on reliability, cost, and delivery time. Unfortunately, this information became less reliable as the Trump administration and the FDA began pursuing out-of-country retailers importing drugs into the US. Beginning in 2019, the FDA started a targeted effort to block online retailers that provided medication abortion pills, sending out warning letters to Rablon, an online pharmacy that provided medication through more than eighty different websites, as well as AidAccess.org, an online medication abortion site operated by Dutch activist Rebecca Gomperts.[50] Rablon ceased operating their sites, and while other pharmacies have stepped in periodically with pills for purchase and import, they are no longer as reliable, and the medications often are held up in customs long enough that they become useless to pregnant people wanting to terminate.

Despite FDA pressure, however, AidAccess.org continues to offer medications in a variety of forms to those seeking them. What medications can be provided depends primarily on where a pregnant person lives and the state laws surrounding the dispensing of mifepristone in that area.

What Is Aid Access?

Aid Access is run by Rebecca Gomperts of Women on Waves/Women on Web. Gomperts is a reproductive rights activist who is already supplying medications in countries where abortion is completely illegal. She believes her actions remain legal because the FDA allows medication to be imported for personal use. Still there are some concerns beyond just the legality, such as the possibility that the medication will not get to a user in a timely manner and before the person is too far along gestationally to use it properly, or that the private information being gathered will somehow be leaked, hacked, or otherwise confiscated and turned over to law enforcement, published online, or in any other way used nefariously. It also must be stressed that in some states, using these medications outside a clinic setting continues to be against the law, even if the importing of the drugs is not.

According to Plan C as of July 2020, "Aid Access is a doctor-supported telemedicine service for self-managed abortion with abortion pills." Aid Access supports people who are not able to access local services. They serve patients who are healthy and less than nine weeks pregnant or have symptoms of a miscarriage.

Depending on where you live, they can offer you different service options.

- In New York and Washington State, Aid Access doctors can provide abortions with the FDA-approved medicines mifepristone and misoprostol, which will arrive within a few days.

- In some US states, Aid Access doctors can provide a prescription for the medicines mifepristone and misoprostol that you can have filled through a trustworthy pharmacy in India. Because of COVID-19, shipments from the pharmacy in India can take up to three weeks to arrive.

- In some other US states, Aid Access doctors can provide medical support for miscarriage management with misoprostol, which is approximately 94 percent effective. You can fill these prescriptions at a US-based online or local pharmacy.

Aid Access's helpdesk and doctor are available to answer any questions before, during, and after the process. Unlike clinic-based medication abortions, Aid Access often charges less than a hundred dollars for the medications.

Why Aren't There More Vendors?

Prior to 2019, one of the most reliable sites for quickly and cheaply obtaining medication abortion was called Macrobiotic Stoner. New Yorker Ursula Wing sold the combo kits online for nearly two years to people who came to her blog—most often through searches on the web. After receiving an order, Wing would place pills inside a piece of hand-made jewelry or some other item from her site, getting them back to the purchaser far more quickly than many options.

However, one person who bought from her was a Wisconsin man who then allegedly used the drugs to try to induce his girlfriend's abortion without her consent. He turned in Wing as his source, and as a result her supplies were seized and Wing was indicted on one count of "conspiracy to defraud various US governmental agencies," fined ten thousand dollars, and put on two years of probation. She also had more than sixty thousand dollars' worth of sales seized by the government.

"Prescription drugs that are obtained illegally from online sources and then sold online to consumers can cause serious harm," said Special Agent in Charge Lynda M. Burdelik, FDA Office of Criminal Investigations, Chicago Field Office, in a July 2020 press release announcing the indictment. "We will continue to investigate and bring justice to those who place the public's health at risk."[51]

How Are Mifepristone and Misoprostol Used to End a Pregnancy?

These instructions are replicated from the Women Help Women website, an open-sourced information-sharing site about World Health Organization protocols (https://consult.womenhelp.org/en/page/401/how-should-i-take-the-pills). Because they are replicated verbatim they contain gendered language.

> These instructions are for a pregnancy that is up to ten weeks (seventy days). The evidence suggests that mifepristone plus misoprostol is very safe and effective to ten weeks. After twelve weeks, there is a higher chance of a complication and the medicines are used differently.
>
> 1. Mifepristone should be swallowed with a glass of water.
> 2. Twenty-four hours later the woman should put four pills of misoprostol buccally (between the gum and the cheek).
>
> She should put two tablets into her mouth, between her gum and cheek, on the left side and two more tablets between the gum and cheek, on the right side.
>
> All four pills should be left in the mouth for approximately thirty minutes to dissolve. Women shouldn't eat or drink anything while the pills are dissolving. Anything left in the mouth after thirty minutes should be swallowed. Before and after using the misoprostol she can eat and drink normally, but should not use drugs or alcohol; she needs to pay attention to her body.

How Is Misoprostol Alone Used to End a Pregnancy?

Again, according to Women Help Women (https://consult.women-help.org/en/page/434/how-should-i-take-the-misoprostol-pills):

These instructions are for a pregnancy that is up to twelve weeks (eighty-four days). These instructions are based on the recommendations of the World Health Organization. After twelve weeks, there is a higher chance of a complication and the medicines are used differently.

A woman will need a total of twelve pills of two hundred micrograms each.

1. A woman should put four pills of two hundred micrograms (in total eight hundred micrograms) misoprostol under the tongue. Do not swallow the pills for at least thirty minutes until the tablets are dissolved! (She can swallow her saliva, but NOT the pills. After thirty minutes it is okay to swallow what remains of the pills.)

2. After three hours she should put another four pills of misoprostol under the tongue. Do not swallow the pills for at least thirty minutes, until the tablets are dissolved.

3. After three hours she should put another four pills of misoprostol under the tongue again for a third time. Do not swallow the pills for at least thirty minutes, until the tablets are dissolved.

In between the doses of misoprostol, a woman can eat and drink normally.

The success rate is approximately 84 percent.

This means that eight to nine women of every ten women who use misoprostol correctly will have a safe abortion after this procedure.

What If There Isn't Much Bleeding?

If a person is using misoprostol alone and does not see any bleeding after their third dose of medication, they may take a fourth dose of four pills under the tongue, following the same procedure as before. This will complete the termination for a majority of those who have not begun to miscarry yet.

How to Know If It Was Successful

A person who successfully managed an induced miscarriage at home would no longer have any signs of pregnancy tissue in an ultrasound five to seven days after the abortion. They should also no longer have a positive pregnancy test four weeks after an abortion. If the abortion was not complete, the person would need to obtain either a vacuum aspiration or more medication depending upon the advancement of the pregnancy at that point.

Medical Risks

According to an article published in the *BMJ* in a study of one thousand women in Ireland who accessed medication abortion via Women on Web (www.womenonweb.org/en/i-need-an-abortion) because abortion was illegal in their country, nearly 95 percent of them were successful in ending their pregnancies without surgical intervention. Less than 10 percent of the patients reported symptoms that were alarming enough to suggest they should seek out medical advice, and there were no deaths.[52]

Public information about potential medical risks and symptoms of a possible complication can be found at the Women Help Women site at https://consult.womenhelp.org/en/page/417/what-to-do-in-case-of-emergency.

The information on the page reads as follows:

Complications after medical abortion are rare, and include

severe bleeding and infection. You should go to the doctor or hospital if you have any of the signs of complication below:

- Severe bleeding (more than two or three pads used every hour for more than two or three hours)
- Severe abdominal pain that isn't relieved with painkillers or continues for two to three days after taking the pills
- Fever over 39° or 38° for more than twenty-four hours (over 101° F)
- Abnormal vaginal discharge

The risk of a complication is low (two to five women in every one hundred), and the need for emergency care (that might be needed in case the woman suffers from heavy bleeding) is extremely low (one in every two thousand women). However, to make the process as safe as possible, it is important to be near medical care in case of an emergency or a complication throughout the process of abortion. If a woman lives far from medical care, she should use the medicines where she can access medical care, preferably within one or two hours. She should also plan how she would get to medical care (by car, taxi, or in case of emergency by ambulance).

If possible, the woman should choose a hospital or doctor where she knows that women having miscarriages are treated respectfully.

If a woman seeks medical attention, she does not have to say she used medicines. She can say she is having a miscarriage. The symptoms and treatment of a complication of miscarriage are exactly the same as those of abortion.

Misoprostol cannot be detected in the blood or any bodily fluids within a few hours after use. Even if a hospital claims that they can check to see if a woman took medicines to cause the miscarriage, it is not true.

How Can Medical Risks Be Minimized?

If a person has begun a self-managed abortion outside a clinical setting and has questions but doesn't want to seek out medical help at this point, there are other options available to them. If they are in the US and need assistance, they can contact:

WOMEN HELP WOMEN
https://abortionpillinfo.org

MISCARRIAGE AND ABORTION (M+A) HOTLINE
https://www.mahotline.org
833-246-2632 (phone or text)

Both sources are completely confidential.

What Should I Expect in a Medication Abortion?

Regardless of whether a person is using mifepristone and misoprostol together, or misoprostol alone, and regardless of whether the medications were purchased from a clinic or another source, the experience will be the same. Medication abortion is an induced miscarriage and as such will involve the same symptoms as a miscarriage: bleeding, pain, and nausea. Just like a miscarriage (and like giving birth, too), there can be a very wide range of physical symptom severity.

While many people are told that a medication abortion will feel much like a "really heavy period," the fact remains that the body is in fact going into labor to expel the pregnancy, and that can be a process that is short or long, mildly painful or excruciating, a period-like amount of blood or a large gush of fluids. Depending on the gestation, the process can be more involved and take more time. A person may see tissue or even the embryo or fetus and its sac, or they may see nothing at all. Vomiting, diarrhea, and gastric issues are a normal part of the experience and nothing to be alarmed about—they are common during miscarriage and birth too. Bleeding heavily is normal, and as long as a person is filling less than two menstrual pads every hour for more than two hours, it is completely fine, unless they are experiencing other symptoms, like a fever, as well.

Can I Do Anything to Make It Easier?

Again, having a medication abortion at home has much in common with having a homebirth, or a miscarriage in your house. But unlike with a homebirth, a person who is managing their own abortion can take Tylenol or another painkiller (just not aspirin, which increases bleeding) an hour before starting misoprostol in order to assist with pain. They are also encouraged to eat and drink lots of fluids, and to be in a place where they are safe and can get as much rest as possible.[53]

Also like a home labor, there are a number of coping techniques. Breathing exercises, yoga stretches, using heating pads, or finding some music, television, or books to pass the time can all help with relaxation and take your mind off discomfort. Having a trusted person with you while you are going through the abortion is always advisable if possible, to provide comfort and support, as well as act as a monitor in the very rare case that there is a medical issue.

What About an Abortion Doula?

As we discussed back in chapter 5, full-spectrum doulas are available to help a person during an abortion—either in a clinic or outside one. For people who are having a medication abortion in private, an abortion doula can offer any type of assistance at any level a pregnant person wants.

Abortion doulas can come to a person's home, or they can provide distance support—which is especially helpful when a person is either not sharing the fact that they are having an abortion with others, or because of quarantine, such as during the COVID-19 pandemic. A remote doula may be able to check in periodically via text or call, asking about pain levels or checking on symptoms like bleeding or nausea. A doula can provide comfort, advice, and support either in person or remotely depending on the need of the pregnant person, and can be on alert to answer questions as they arise during the process. Like any other medical provider, a verified, full-spectrum doula would not breach patient confidentiality if medications being used did not come from an abortion clinic or authorized dispenser.

If you are considering managing your own medication abortion at home and want personal support during the process—regardless of how you obtain pills—consider using the list of full-spectrum doula resources earlier in the book.

Legal Risks

There are multiple legal risks that can come with self-inducing an abortion, and not just for the person who is terminating the pregnancy.

Even with *Roe* in place, nearly two dozen people have been jailed for various crimes associated with allegedly inducing abortions, ranging from murder, homicide, and feticide to failure to report a death or properly dispose of remains, child endangerment or negligence, and being in possession of a drug without a prescription.

Unsurprisingly, it is people of color who tend to get the most severe punishments. Because prosecutors and other law enforcement officials typically pursue the "crime" of self-induced abortion at their discretion, racial bias becomes a large factor in deciding who should be investigated and to what extent they should be charged.

"Whether they are choosing to end a pregnancy or continue one, low-income women and women of color are more likely to be the target of investigations and prosecutions, as they are less likely to be able to access private medical care and more likely to regularly encounter police and other government officials in their day-to-day lives. In the post-*Roe* world, women themselves, and low-income women and women of color in particular, are at more risk of criminal prosecution for abortion and other pregnancy outcomes than at any other point in history," explains the National Institute for Reproductive Health in their report, *When Self-Abortion is a Crime: Laws That Put Women at Risk.*[54]

Those who may be seen as "assisting" in a self-induced abortion could face charges as well. One Pennsylvania mother was jailed for providing abortion-inducing medications to her daughter because there was no nearby clinic.[55] Other potential charges could include "unlawful termination of pregnancy" for someone who may live at the same address or whose computer or phone was used to purchase medicines, or "accessory" charges if they are found to have helped cover up an illegal abortion during an investigation.

According to the Self-Induced Abortion (SIA) Legal Team report *Roe's Unfinished Promise*, "There are seven states with laws directly criminalizing self-induced abortions, ten states with laws criminalizing harm to fetuses that lack adequate exemptions for the pregnant person, and fifteen states with criminal abortion laws that have been and could be misapplied to people who self-induce. There are also a number of laws deployed when no other legal authorization to punish can be found (obscure laws like disposal of human remains or concealing a birth), which have led to at least twenty arrests for [self-induced abortion] and criminal investigations in twenty states for alleged self-induced abortions since 1973."[56]

There is little doubt that as abortion becomes more illegal and inaccessible, more people will go to jail if they are discovered conducting or assisting in a self-managed abortion. If you need legal help or wish to support those who will assist in legal defense for these cases, consider reaching out to the Self-Induced Abortion (SIA) Legal Team, a part of If/When/How's Lawyering Project:

REPRO LEGAL HELPLINE
844-868-2812 (legal help line)
https://www.reprolegalhelpline.org/contact-the-helpline/#secure-form

What People Self-Managing Their Abortion Need to Know

While the laws differ from state to state and will get even more extreme as *Roe* is dismantled and potentially overturned, none of this will change the fact that being able to determine your own medical care—including if and when you want to carry a pregnancy to term—is a human right. That also includes a person's right to health care for whatever that person's circumstances warrant. No person should ever feel the need to avoid follow-up care because of fear of an arrest. According to a video on the SIA website:

- A person has the right to talk to a health care provider before, during, and after a self-managed abortion—but they also have the right to provide as much or as little detail as they choose.
- That includes hospital staff, emergency room doctors, and anyone else who may ask questions about recent medical actions.
- Doctors state that there is no difference between how they treat complications from a miscarriage and how they treat complications from an abortion, meaning there is no need for a person to clarify which may be occurring.
- Doctors admit there is no actual test that can show if a person has ingested medications meant to induce a miscarriage.
- There are no laws that require hospitals to report suspected abortions to law enforcement.
- Some states even impose penalties on health care providers who violate a person's privacy by releasing personal health information without patient consent.
- However, because not all medical professionals are clear on the laws, or on the importance of maintaining doctor/patient confidentiality, a patient should always only provide the information they feel comfortable with sharing.

We will discuss how to minimize other potential legal risks in greater detail in chapter 10.

Can People Share Information About Using Abortion Pills?

While conducting an abortion outside a clinic setting may not be legal in all circumstances, sharing open-sourced information is always legal. Please be aware that this is publicly available information based on the World Health Organization (WHO) protocol, and is not meant to encourage a person to induce a termination of pregnancy.

ReproAction has been leading the charge to make sure Self-Managed Abortion (SMA) information is shared as publicly and clearly as possible. Their campaign to demystify and destigmatize medication abortion outside a clinic setting includes providing easily accessible and understandable graphics explaining the procedure, its minimal risks, and why it should be widely available. The following has been reprinted with permission. You can download your own copies at https://reproaction.org/wp-content/uploads/2017/05/About-SMA-with-pills-Factsheet.pdf and distribute them personally with no fear of prosecution.

Chapter 8 Worksheet

Preparing for an At-Home Abortion

Regardless of whether you are using medications from a clinic, a telemedicine prescription, or another source, a home abortion is a process you want to prepare for ahead of time. Here's how to get ready.

1) *Pick a day.*

You will want to be sure to choose a day when you won't be interrupted. The process could take as long as twenty-four hours from the time you start the procedure. Make sure you won't have to deal with obligations like work, school, or child/eldercare if at all possible.

Facts about Misoprostol for

SELF-MANAGED ABORTION

Everyone has the right to information about how misoprostol is used to safely and effectively end a pregnancy. Consciousness-raising is the first step in making medications like misoprostol available to any pregnant person legally, affordably, and conveniently.

No method of self-managed abortion should be shamed, and certainly not criminalized.

Misoprostol is typically used within the first 12 weeks of pregnancy and is about 85 percent effective.

The World Health Organization recommends that people who want to manage their abortion via misoprostol take a total of 12 tablets (200 mcg each). These tablets are administered four at a time, under the tongue, and allowed to dissolve for 30 minutes, every three hours.

Normal side effects of misoprostol include: cramps, bleeding, nausea, vomiting, diarrhea, and chills. Though very rare, signs of potential complications that should be treated at a hospital include: heavy bleeding that lasts for more than two hours, high fever, and severe pain.

Abortion with pills taken orally presents like a miscarriage. There is no need to disclose use of pills to medical staff because it may be legally risky. At least 20 women have been arrested for ending their pregnancies.

Self-managed abortion may be a first choice for some and a last resort for others. Either way, pregnant people should be able to have an abortion on their own terms – whether that is at a clinic or in the privacy of their own home.

Get involved with

Reproaction

www.reproaction.org

For information on self-managed abortion using mifepristone and misoprostol or more on the WHO protocols for misoprostol alone, see our other fact sheets available on our website.

2) *Prepare your space.*

Pull together anything you might want for comfort. Make sure you have enough food, plenty to drink (but not alcohol), plenty of pads (no tampons or cups), pain killers (no aspirin), anti-nausea medicine, and a heating pad. Pull together any distractions you might want, like music, candles, calming scents, movies, books, or magazines.

3) *Find a helper.*

You probably don't want to be alone during this process. If you have someone you can trust—a friend, a partner, a family member—invite them to stay with you, even if you don't want them in the room with you. At the very least have someone who will periodically check in with you to anchor you and follow your progress. If you don't have someone you trust, consider reaching out to an abortion doula.

4) *Pick out some clothes, blankets, and towels.*

You want to be comfortable. You should also recognize that whatever you wear may end up unusable by the end of the day. Make sure you protect any furniture or other items ahead of time with blankets or towels. It's always better to be safe than sorry.

5) *Prepare some DIY labor tools.*

A tennis ball is great for squeezing when you have a cramp. A sock filled with rice that has been heated in the microwave for two minutes is a fabulous makeshift heating pad. A miscarriage is a mini-labor, so feel free to treat it like one and use every tool you can.

6) *Buy some extra pregnancy tests.*

If you aren't intending to follow up with a medical provider, be sure to have some pregnancy tests on hand to determine if the abortion was successful. You should no longer test positive four weeks after your abortion, although in rare cases some people still show a positive for another two to four weeks. If you are still having positive tests and experiencing pregnancy symptoms, be sure to see a doctor for testing.

7) *Have a plan for an emergency.*

It is very, very unlikely that you will have a medical issue, but it's always good to have a plan just in case. Should you have a fever over 102 degrees, bleed so much that you are soaking more than two pads an hour for more than two hours, or have severe pain that doesn't respond to pain medication, you may need to visit a hospital. If you do and your abortion drugs were not from a legal provider, remember that all you need to say to a doctor is "I'm pregnant. I think I'm having a miscarriage," and "I'm scared." Medication will not show up in your bloodstream or in any urine tests, and your miscarriage looks no different from one that occurred naturally.

So You Want to Be the Next "Jane"

"Bring back Jane!"

That has been the call of many abortion supporters since hearing Trump would get to add another justice bent on ending legal abortion to the Supreme Court. Luckily, abortion techniques have vastly progressed since the Janes were providing illegal abortions in the late 1960s and early '70s. That means people seeking to end their pregnancies outside a clinic setting are far more likely to turn to medications than medical devices.

Yet there will probably always be some people looking for ways to terminate a pregnancy without the use of medications. This chapter provides information on menstrual extractions and early vacuum aspirations for those who are truly insistent on "bringing back Jane" and offering non-medication abortion outside a legal clinical setting.

Who Was "Jane"?

The Jane Collective was a group of mostly white women from the Chicago area who first offered counseling and referrals and later trained to provide first- and second-trimester abortions prior to legalization in 1973. The Janes—all in their late teens and twenties—started out by using doctors or other medical professionals and simply acting as the go-between for pregnant people and the providers, but they eventually realized that they could easily do D&Cs (dilation and curettage, where the cervix is opened with dilators then the uterus is gently scraped with an instrument to remove the embryo or fetus as well as additional products of conception like placenta and uterine lining) themselves. This offered them not just a chance to eliminate how many people were involved that could be susceptible to a police investigation, but also to do lower-cost and even free abortions since there was no doctor to pay.

The Janes were forced to work under multiple layers of secrecy to protect themselves and their patients from the law. They shared a phone number through posters, fliers, and word of mouth, telling people who were pregnant and didn't want to be to call and leave a callback number, as well as the date of their last period. The Janes would return calls afterward with instructions on where to meet. The meeting area was just the first step—the patient would then wait for transportation to another secret location, and it was there that the abortion would be performed.

Most of the Janes had no professional medical background. Instead, they learned first from their original doctors and then later from each other. According to NPR, which profiled the Jane Collective in an article in early 2018, the group believes they performed about eleven thousand first- and second-trimester abortions in the four years they operated before the *Roe* decision came down and abortion was legalized in the country.[57]

For more information about the Janes, read Laura Kaplan's book *The Story of Jane: The Legendary Underground Feminist Abortion Service*. Kaplan, a former Jane, provides a fascinating look into the history and legacy of the radical group—one that is even more compelling as the country returns to a pre-*Roe* era.

How Were Abortions Done Pre-Roe?

The coat hanger became and for some reason remains the ubiquitous symbol of the illegal abortion, and it's true that some women may have used that, but it was just one of many ways that pregnant people attempted to end their pregnancies pre-*Roe*.

Kate Manning, author of *My Notorious Life*, highlighted many of the most popular pre-*Roe* home abortion remedies in a *New York Times* column in 2013. "WHY would a woman put a leech inside her body, in the most private of female places? Why would she put cayenne pepper there? Why might a woman swallow lye? Gunpowder? Why would a woman hit herself about the abdomen with a meat pulverizer? A brickbat? Throw herself down the stairs? Why would she syringe herself, internally, with turpentine? Gin? Drink laundry bluing? Why might she probe herself with a piece of whalebone? A turkey feather? A knitting needle? Why would she consume medicine made of pulverized Spanish fly? How about powdered ergot, a poisonous fungus? Or strychnine, a poison? Why would she take a bath in scalding water? Or spend the night in the snow?" Manning asked. "Because she wanted to end a pregnancy. Historically, women have chosen all those methods to induce abortion."[58]

While dangerous DIY home abortion approaches using tools, corrosives, and toxins were commonplace before *Roe* (and unfortunately are still attempted in times of complete desperation today, as we learned from the 2015 arrest of a woman who tried to do her own abortion at home using a coat hanger[59]) so were actual medical procedures done by trained professionals and even enthusiastic activists.

D&C abortion was how the women of Jane performed their abortions, but other activists also worked outside the medical profession complex and offered abortions via menstrual extractions—a type of early manual vacuum aspiration.

Unlike a D&C, menstrual extractions didn't require that the cervix be dilated, making it far simpler for someone without extensive medical training to perform them. Because there is no curettage, there is less likelihood of a hemorrhage or puncture, too.

In California, a group of women began meeting to conduct "self-help clinics" to do menstrual extractions, teaching each other to insert speculums and look at their own cervixes. Soon after, they adapted a manual aspirator that would allow them to essentially suction out menstrual lining and blood all at once at the beginning of a period, or, if a period was delayed because of possible early pregnancy, simply remove the lining and fertilized egg all at once.

The tool and technique was developed by Carol Downer and Lorraine Rothman, who took a standard plastic cannula and syringe, then modified it in order to ensure there would be enough container for a full menses to fit in and that there would be no issue with air accidentally being pumped back into the uterus, where it could cause a potential embolism. With their new kits they believed they could do extraction and very early abortion in a safer, less uncomfortable manner, eliminating the sharp tools and the lack of anesthetic that came from traditional illegal D&Cs, where abortion providers refused to give patients medications so they could leave more quickly if there were police or other problems.

What to Know About Menstrual Extraction

The process is done with a device called a Del Em, which nonmedical professionals have been able to build at home. According to Carol Downer, one of the originators of the American practice, menstrual extraction should always be done with others, and never on yourself. "The tabloids and the electronic media have labeled menstrual extraction 'self-abortion' or 'do-it-yourself abortion' but these terms are misleading," Downer explains in her 1992 book *A Woman's Book of Choices: Abortion, Menstrual Extraction, RU-486*, coauthored with Rebecca Chalker. "First of all, due to the location of the uterus, it is virtually impossible for a woman to do ME on herself. To do the procedure safely and correctly, a woman needs the help of one or more women who are trained and experienced in ME."

Other practitioners disagree with Downer's conclusion, stating they have had success learning to perform ME on their own bodies, using additional mirrors and bright lamps in order to better examine themselves.

The most significant physical risk of menstrual extraction is the possibility of infection from unsterile equipment or otherwise introducing bacteria into the uterus. Downer suggests in her book that a person doing menstrual extractions do them multiple times on non-pregnant people in order to gain experience before ever attempting it on a person who may be pregnant.

How Can a Person Build a Del Em?

Below is an image of items needed for crafting the Del Em, provided by Carol Downer via her website Women's Health Specialists (https://www.womenshealthspecialists.org/self-help/menstrual-extraction/).

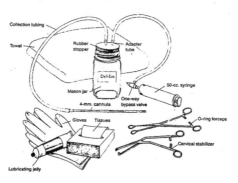

What Are the Instructions for Doing a Menstrual Extraction?

A person can easily find instructions for doing a menstrual extraction online. Full information, including illustrations, is available at http://womenshealthinwomenshands.com/PDFs/MenstrualExtraction.pdf, which is a reprint of the detailed guide published in *A New View of Women's Bodies*, a now out-of-print book published by the Federation of Women's Health Centers in 1981.

The following information was found at http://www.skepticfiles.org/atheist2/selfabor.htm and was allegedly first published in a pamphlet called *Womenpower—Do It Yourself Abortion—Time's Up!*

How to Perform a Menstrual Extraction (ME)

1) Supplies first: Betadine, speculum, "Del Em" ME equipment, latex gloves, alcohol, Valerian or Motrin, copy of *When Birth Control Fails*, small four millimeter and five millimeter cannulas, flashlight, mirror, pillows.

2) Before proceeding, with the help of your group, check to see if you're pregnant or not. ME can be done on nonpregnant women. Look at your cervix and see if it has changed in color or texture. Have a member of your self-help group perform a pelvic exam as well. Make sure it is someone who has felt your cervix before. See if your cervix feels enlarged or softer to her. Have you had any morning sickness? For how long? Study your most recent menstrual cycle. You do this by counting the number of weeks that have passed since your last normal period. If you are late, this might be a sign

that you are pregnant. If you think you might be more than eight weeks pregnant, *do not* proceed with this method.

3) Lie back on a low bed or futon and, with your legs spread, get comfortable. You may want someone to hold your legs for you. Definitely have someone by your side to assist you with whatever you might want (water, abdominal massage, Motrin, an extra pillow) during the extraction.

4) Although the vagina is not a sterile area, bacteria should never enter the os, cervix, or uterus or else you run the risk of infection. With the speculum in place, so that your cervix can be easily seen by the person who will be holding the cannula, and using tongs that have been boiled until sterile to hold a Betadine soaked cotton swab, cleanse the cervix and the vaginal canal.

5) Touching only the two or so inches furthest from the end of the cannula that will enter the cervix, carefully put the cannula inside the vagina (do not let it touch the vaginal walls either; remember the vagina is not a sterile field) and slowly insert it into the exterior os. After you have put the cannula into the os about three-quarters of an inch, you will begin to feel resistance, as if the cannula will not go any further. You have reached the inner os or the entrance to the uterus. You may feel cramping at this point because both the os and the uterus are muscles. The uterus may also recede into the body making it hard to continue. This is normal as well. Continue to push, with a gentle insistence, until you feel something give and the level of resistance reduce; the cannula has entered the uterus.

6) It is time to attach the rest of the Del Em apparatus to the cannula. Before doing so, remove all the air from a Del Em jar using your one-way valve syringe. This will provide the right amount of suction needed to detach early-first-trimester menses and fetal tissue from the uterine wall. Attach the tubing to the cannula and begin to move it in a semi-slow, back-and-forth rotating fashion in the uterus. Remain in one area until you feel the texture of the uterus go from soft and mushy to hard and ribbed or ridge-like. Then repeat the same motions in another part of the uterus. You will see blood and, if you are pregnant, a white, pudding-like substance (fetal tissue) in the tubing. Continue to do this until you no longer feel (through your "eleventh finger," the cannula) any softness in the uterus nor see any blood or fetal tissue in the tubing. Remove the cannula. Mission accomplished.

Where Can I Find the Tools for Making a Del Em?

Many of the tools can be found through medical supply stores. One woman, meanwhile, provides her own experience online on her blog of building one at home and for minimal cost primarily by obtaining items from local stores and a pet supply company. Writing at the *Reproductive Right Blog* (the-reproductive-right.blogspot.com) the woman explains that after purchasing a speculum off eBay, she then found the rest of the supplies much closer to home, including a mason jar, a rubber sink stopper, tubing, and a one-way value in a pet store's fish department, and a spray bottle tube for a cannula. She then bought a meat injector and removed the needle to serve as her syringe. Cut down the stopper if it is too large for the jar, she writes, then create two small holes for the tubing. After inserting the tubing and creating an airtight seal around the holes, add the valve to one end and then the syringe. Add the cannula to the other and test your device on a glass of water to be certain it works, she advises.[60]

What's a Manual Vacuum Aspiration?

A manual vacuum aspiration (MVA) is similar to a menstrual extraction but can be done until later gestation (usually up to fourteen weeks). Unlike a menstrual extraction, a series of dilators is used to slowly and incrementally open the cervix, allowing a larger cannula to be inserted, which by extension means a more developed pregnancy can be terminated in this manner.

The following instructions are meant only for trained medical professionals and were found in Médecins Sans Frontières (MSF), which "has been producing medical guides for over twenty-five years to help practitioners in the field. The contents of these guides are based on scientific data collected from MSF's experience, the World Health Organization (WHO), other renowned international medical institutions and medical and scientific journals." The instructions can be found at https://medicalguidelines.msf.org/viewport/EONC/english/9-5-manual-vacuum-aspiration-mva-20316948.html, under the section "9.5 Manual Vacuum Aspiration." Instructions pick up after placing the speculum in the patient.

Dilation

Dilate the cervix if the cervical canal cannot accommodate the cannula appropriate for gestational age (or the size of the uterus). Dilation should be smooth and gradual:

—With one hand, pull the forceps attached to the cervix and keep traction in order to bring the cervix and the uterine body into the best possible alignment.

—With the other hand, insert the smallest diameter dilator; then switch to the next larger dilator. Continue in this way, using the next size dilator each time, until obtaining dilation appropriate to the cannula to be inserted, without ever relaxing the traction on the cervix.

—Insert the dilator through the internal os. A resistance may be felt: this indicates that there is no need to advance the dilator any further. This resistance is not necessarily felt. In such case, it can be assumed that the internal os has been penetrated when the dilator has been inserted five centimeters beyond the external os.

—Do not force the cervix with the dilators (risk of rupture or perforation, especially when the uterus is very retro- or anteverted).

Aspiration

—Attach the prepared (i.e., under vacuum) sterile syringe to the chosen cannula.

—Maintain traction on the cervix with one hand.

—With the other hand, gently insert the cannula into the uterine cavity. Rotating the cannula while applying gentle pressure facilitates insertion. Slowly and cautiously push the cannula into the uterine cavity until it touches the fundus.

—Release the valves on the syringe to perform the aspiration. The contents of the uterus should be visible through the syringe (blood and the whitish products of conception).

—Hold the syringe by the tube (not the plunger) once a

vacuum has been established in the syringe and the cannula has been inserted into the uterus; otherwise, the plunger can go back in, pushing the aspirated tissue or air back into the uterus.

—Carefully (risk of perforation) suction all areas of the uterus, gently rotating the cannula back and forth 180°. Take care not to break the vacuum by pulling the cannula out of the uterine cavity.

—If the syringe is full, close the valves, disconnect the syringe from the cannula, empty the contents, re-establish the vacuum, and reconnect the syringe to the cannula and continue the procedure.

—Stop when the uterus is empty, as indicated by a foamy, reddish-pink aspirate, with no tissue in the syringe. It is also possible to assess the emptiness of the uterus by passing the cannula over the surface of the uterus: if the surface feels rough, or it feels as if the uterus is contracting around the cannula, assume that the evacuation is complete.

—Close the valve, detach the syringe and then remove the cannula and the forceps. Check for bleeding before removing the speculum.

In a surgical setting, aspiration can be done using a cannula connected to the electric suction machine, with a maximum pressure of eight hundred millibars.

Examining the aspirated contents

To confirm that the uterus has been emptied, check the presence and quantity of debris, estimating whether it corresponds to the gestational age.

The debris consists of villi, fetal membranes, and, beyond nine weeks, fetal fragments. To inspect the tissues visually, place them in a compress or strainer, and rinse them with water.

Where Would I Find Equipment if I Wanted to Perform MVA?

Because MVA should only be conducted by trained professionals, most equipment can only be found through medical retailers. There are rare occasions that abortion tools can be discovered in places like rummage shops or other unique stores (for example, I found dilators and a speculum at an art fair in a "Strange Items" boutique display).

MVA kits can also be purchased through some websites, which can be found by googling keywords like "Menstrual extraction kits" or "MVA kits" or "MVA tools." One such complete kit was found on the online retail site https://www.alibaba.com, which offers disposable MVA kits for anywhere between ten and fifty dollars apiece, depending on the number purchased. Note: this retailer has not been verified; this is only an explanation of how a person would find kits online.

What Are the Risks of Doing Non-Medication Abortion Outside Clinics?

According to the Janes, they never had a patient die, but they did have to occasionally send them to the emergency room for follow-up care—dealing with complications that included excessive bleeding or incomplete abortion. Of course that was fifty years ago, and using a curettage, which is not in any of the practices above.

Still, unlike medication-induced abortion, these other procedures introduce obvious medical risks. Not having properly and completely sterilized equipment means a possibility of bacterial infection even if the abortion itself is a complete success, and few people have antibiotics just lying around for treatment. While a medication abortion can be done solely by the pregnant person if they choose, these non-medication techniques require at least one other person to be involved in the procedure, opening up more legal risks, too. And while medication abortion doesn't require any experience, MVA and even menstrual extraction requires extensive practice to complete safely, something that would be difficult to obtain outside a medical setting.

Are MVA and ME safer than introducing a long, sharp object into the womb through the cervix in order to start a miscarriage? Or ingesting toxic poisons or inserting them into the uterus? No doubt. But with medications in existence that can safely be used to end a pregnancy, "safer than douching with lye" really shouldn't be our standard anymore.

If a person were to decide to try to undertake abortion outside a legal clinic setting after the first trimester, the simplest and least dangerous way to undertake that process would simply be to attempt a miscarriage with the same medications used for medication abortion. The major difference between the protocol earlier in the pregnancy and later in the pregnancy would be the amount of time and medication necessary, and the amount of support a person would require to go through the abortion.

One abortion provider with over twenty years of experience suggested that in their opinion mifepristone and misoprostol alone in multiple doses would work. In such a situation, a person would want to take one dose of mifepristone, then wait thirty-six hours, then take four hundred micrograms of misoprostol every three hours until completion. This method would likely be able to end a pregnancy at any gestation. Also, according to them, this would be the "the safest route to go" if the options are using medication or attempting an invasive procedure outside a clinic setting. They suggested having an experienced doula involved as a support person in this case to assist with the process.

How Can I Find Abortion Assistance Outside of Traditional Medical Practices?

Probably the biggest question anyone will be asking if *Roe* is overturned is "Where can I go to get a safe abortion?" Luckily, there are variety of people who have already been practicing reproductive health care for decades (or in some cases centuries) outside of the traditional medical lanes.

Just like the early feminist health centers that used to meet and perform menstrual extractions, today there are pockets of "radical" community health care workers who are working to create patient-centered and empowered medical care outside a mainstream medical practice.

One particular curriculum along that line is "autonomous pelvic care," which was developed by an activist in the Appalachian area.

Centered on "people with uteruses," autonomous pelvic care creates a non-judgmental, non-procedural series of reproductive interventions that are trans- and queer-inclusive and holistic rather than pharmaceutical in nature. It involves "menstrual support and regulation," herbal remedies for common pelvic complaints, and self-managed abortion care. Autonomous pelvic care inspires medical treatment that is directed and performed by the patient, usually in a home environment rather than an office or medical center.

"Seeking treatment for common pelvic (reproductive and sexual) ailments under the white supremacist bio-medical patriarchy can be difficult and traumatizing for many," explains Mountain Access Brigade (MAB), a radical health care collective, in a description of their Common Pelvic Ailments and Infections Day Camp. "There are multiple ailments which are often best treated by ourselves at home, and understanding symptoms and treatment is crucial to staying out of the gynecologist's office. This workshop covers a historical look at STIs and STI stigma, an overview of self-managed care, identifying and treating common ailments (including yeast infections, bacterial vaginosis, and urinary tract infections), at-home STI testing, and so on."

Like their Common Pelvic Ailments and Infections Day Camp,

MAB's Self-Managed Abortion class offers historic and legal information about self-managed care, security and privacy protocols, and a "tincture" making guide. Altogether, Autonomous Pelvic Care seeks to "empower self-directed decision making and community-based provision of care, focusing on queer-positive, anti-racist liberation and support."

For more information on how to sign up for a workshop, contact autonomouspelviccare@protonmail.com.

Papaya Workshops

Meanwhile, if you are determined to learn how to provide non-medication-based abortions outside a medical setting—despite knowing the physical and legal dangers of doing so—one place to learn how is exactly the same place abortion providers have been doing so for ages: a Papaya Workshop.

Developed by the Bixby Center for Global Reproductive Health at the University of California, San Francisco, as part of its Innovating Education in Reproductive Health program, the Papaya Workshop teaches new to abortion care students how to safely perform manual uterine aspiration, both as a means of offering abortion itself and for providing follow-up care for missed miscarriages or incomplete medication abortions.

Because a papaya so closely replicates the size and shape of a typical uterus, students are able to use the fruit to simulate giving an injection into the cervix and then aspirating the uterus using a manual, non-electric aspirator. The training also covers how to insert an IUD after an aspiration.

The workshop has been conducted in non-medical spaces, as well, including at reproductive rights and justice conferences and even the progressive Netroots Nation conference (although a national papaya recall forced workshop leaders to improvise with a watermelon instead).[61]

Even journalists with no medical background have found the session useful. "[The instructor] held the papaya for me and after I dilated it, she reminded me how to attach the aspirator to the cannula. I clamped down the two small locks on the end of the instrument, pulled the handle toward me to create suction, and eased it gently onto the plastic tube—I wasn't going to be the one to perforate my papaya's fundus," wrote VICE News' Marie Solis, who attended a New York workshop in 2019.

"In one smooth motion, I rotated the aspirator, drawing out dozens of seeds, surprised and pleased to see that my amateur skills could produce the same result. Next to me, others were doing the same, rejoicing with every successful extraction."[62]

For more information on the Papaya Workshops visit https://papayaworkshop.org/.

Can I Get Arrested for Providing an Abortion if I'm Not a Doctor?

Yes. Absolutely. Even with abortion legal, abortion opponents are fiercely charging those who help a person end a pregnancy outside an approved clinical setting. Jennifer Whalen's 2014 arrest for helping her daughter obtain medicine to end her pregnancy put her in jail with a felony for "offering medical consultation about abortion without a medical license" as well as misdemeanors for endangering the welfare of a child, dispensing drugs without being a pharmacist, and assault.

According to the *New York Times* in 2014, "In thirty-nine states, it's against the law to perform an abortion if you're not a doctor. In some of the remaining states, you are still required to be a medical professional (a midwife, nurse, or physician assistant). In New York, you can do your own abortion in the first two trimesters, but only if you're following a doctor's advice. About a quarter of states also still have old laws that make it a crime to help someone else with a self-induction. In a law passed in 1845, for example, Massachusetts calls for a sentence of up to seven years for assisting."[63]

Massachusetts revoked their law in the summer of 2018 and New York is currently looking to remove theirs as well. But be certain that when *Roe* falls, wherever abortion is made illegal, the biggest focus will be on arresting those who provide clandestine abortions. That means increased legal danger for anyone helping a person obtain medicines, assisting in non-medication procedures, or helping minors bypass laws around parental consent.

With this risk in mind, the next chapter will discuss tactics for keeping your actions secure and private.

Chapter 9 Worksheet
Becoming a Non-Traditional Abortion Provider

1) *Decide if this is the right role for you to undertake at this moment.* In the worst-case scenario, you will be discovered and potentially jailed. Run through the checklist in chapter 7's "Is Civil Disobedience Right for You?" and be certain you have examined the impact arrest would have on you, your family, and anyone else in your community who may be affected.

2) *Familiarize yourself with the various methods available.* If you

are considering herbal procedures, become familiar with the recipes provided in chapter 8 or consider one of the autonomous pelvic care trainings. If you believe you will want to provide menstrual extractions, find a person or people who menstruate who are willing to allow you to practice on them, or set up properly to practice on yourself. If you are determined to do MVA, attend a Papaya Workshop and practice repeatedly prior to the procedure. Remember that medical students who learn abortion techniques often do them dozens or even hundreds of times before they start work at clinics.

3) *Talk to friends you trust.* Once you feel completely comfortable and are certain you have the skills to perform an abortion without endangering anyone, you might find yourself tempted to offer care to those who are pregnant and can't access a legal abortion provider. Again, this service is illegal in many states, and this checklist should not be considered a recommendation to break the law. If a person chose to carry on despite this warning, they would most likely look to their own trusted friend group first as a way to inform those in need that services exist. Currently, one in four people capable of becoming pregnant have had abortions, and odds are that rate won't go down even if abortion becomes illegal. After all, we've seen repeatedly in the US and elsewhere that people will continue to terminate pregnancies—legal or not. If a person still chose to take this path despite knowing the legal implications, that person would need to be EXTREMELY certain they could trust the friends in question. Review the suggestions about forming a "network of trust" in chapter 10 for advice on staying safe and secure once abortion is illegal.

4) *Reach out to full-spectrum doulas.* If anyone would know how to get a procedural abortion should they become illegal, it would

be your local doula groups. They may or may not be able to provide information (both for legal and safety reasons) but would be the first line that pregnant people would seek out if they wanted care outside a clinic setting. Do not expect it to be easy to develop a relationship with a full-spectrum doula group—especially not in an abortion-hostile state—but if you are determined to provide services yourself, you should be willing to build a long-term relationship of trust with these groups.

5) *Consider guerrilla promotion.* Finally, if you really want to go old-school "Jane," then promote yourself. Just as original pre-*Roe* Janes worked off a private phone number spread word-of-mouth or passed hand-to-hand on slips of paper, a modern Jane could self-promote with stickers on lampposts or bathroom doors and an anonymous e-mail account. Just remember to stay completely untraceable, and treat every person who contacts you as someone likely trying to put you—and all illegal abortion providers—in jail.

Avoiding Surveillance in a Post-*Roe* America

Even with abortion technically legal in the United States, those who terminate their pregnancies outside the inconsistent and often medically unnecessary governmental parameters can find themselves facing time in jail. As more states add more barriers—or end legal abortion altogether—that rate of prosecution will only increase.

In an age of endless information on the Internet and social media channels that can reach across state lines and around the globe, it is easier than ever to find information, medication, and other forms of medical assistance if you want to end a pregnancy or help someone who needs an abortion. But that's a double-edged sword, too, since it's also much easier to find evidence to prosecute someone who is working outside the officially sanctioned rules for termination.

This chapter is all about how to stay secure when it comes to finding abortion information, self-managing abortion care, or assisting someone else in terminating a pregnancy. It also includes safety tips for those who may be setting up new activist organizations in underserved areas of the US, or for those who may want to donate or be involved with organizations but don't want to be identified as supporters.

How to Have an Abortion without
Leaving an Electronic Trail

Not leaving an electronic trail when researching or obtaining an abortion isn't just something for a person to consider once abortion is illegal. For a significant number of pregnant people, even obtaining a legal abortion is something they would like to keep as private as possible, and they may prefer not to have a partner, friends, or family members know about the pregnancy or procedure.

In January 2017, the *Cut*'s Lisa Ryan wrote a very detailed article called "How to Plan an Abortion in the Surveillance State," that offers a number of best practices that could be used regardless of a person's reason for wanting to keep their abortion a secret.

Ryan suggests simple steps like "Don't send private messages on your work computer" or "Get a disposable phone" and recommends using encrypted texting apps like Signal—which you can set to wipe your text messages after a certain period of time so they cannot be used as evidence later on. You can also create a separate, secret e-mail that will only be used for arranging the abortion, or even better, do everything offline to be sure that there is no electronic trail at all. She also advises using a completely private browser like Tor, which passes your search through multiple servers, making it far more difficult for someone to track your search engine history or browsing activity.[64]

Using Your Phone as Your Go-To Tool

Of course, if it comes to seeking an abortion or organizing to help others do so, it would be almost impossible to do absolutely everything offline. In that case, it may work best to use your phone as your sole tool—from secure texting and phone calls via Signal to web browsing only on your smartphone (and on public Wi-Fi) and creating separate e-mail addresses that all can be accessed via mobile. There is some benefit to keeping everything all in one place—especially if you keep your phone secure and clear your cache frequently in case of anyone searching your phone or, even worse, police seizing it.

Here are some tips on good phone security practices taken from both the ACLU's "Freedom of the Press Foundation"[65] and a cybersecurity specialist who works in abortion access spaces. These tips offer good advice for anyone who needs extra security from potential government surveillance.

Encrypt your phone. Having an encrypted phone means that your data will not be readable to anyone when your phone is powered down, and even if a copy is made of your phone data, it won't be readable without your code. This requires using a pin or pass phrase to unlock your device, which might seem like a lot of work at first, but it's worth it, and you will get used to it. iPhones and other Apple mobile devices are encrypted by default. For Androids and other devices, go to the "privacy and security" sections of their settings. Note that encrypting your phone may put it out of commission for ten to thirty minutes during setup.

Lock your phone with a complex pass code. Change your settings so your phone locks immediately after sleep, and immediately after you press the power button. While this doesn't encrypt your phone (it's always unencrypted while it's on, especially on Android), it will prevent anyone from accessing and using your apps. It's not recommended that you use fingerprint, face ID, or anything biometric to lock your phone—facial recognition can be tricked with some photos, fingerprints hacked remotely, and police don't need permission to unlock a phone using biometrics.[66]

Prevent your SMS apps from showing the full text of a message while the phone is locked. No one should be able to read your communications with friends, or two-factor authentication codes, without opening the app first. These can be found in the "notifications" section of most phones' settings.

Lock your SIM card. Set a PIN to control access to your SIM data and cellular network use. A SIM card may still be unlocked by your carrier, but locking it locally protects against people who grab your card from you.

Practice good login hygiene. Use strong pass phrases, two-factor authentication, and different passwords for different accounts with the help of a password manager.

Protect your mobile service account. Take the time to properly lock down the account you have with your mobile carrier. Some people think of it as an afterthought, but it's alarmingly easy for anyone to take over your phone number, SIM card, and eventually, all mobile communications if such accounts aren't secured. Visit your provider's website to create a strong pass phrase and/or backup PIN for your account. Then call your provider and have a representative put a "security notice" on your account, saying something to the effect of "No one can make any changes to my account unless they give you the pass phrase/PIN first."

Limit porting requests on your phone number. Call your phone carrier and ask them to limit or lock out porting requests on your number, preventing someone else from putting in a request that would forward your messages to their phone.

Keep a list of all the accounts that are important to you. Having a list of accounts that need to be addressed in the event of compromise will save you time and worry.

Burst the cloud! Frequently delete your browsing history from your web browsing apps via their settings. If you're a Google services user, prune (or better yet, disable) your "web and web activity." iPhone users must prevent messaging apps from syncing data to iCloud. We know it might seem scary, but unlinking your phone and mac computers from iCloud is the best way to protect your data from prying eyes. Journalists, activists, and concerned citizens usually want to sync photos and videos to the cloud as soon as they take them, and that's okay! However, consider using another cloud-based service that gives you more control over how, when, and where you sync your data—something better than iCloud.

Use good device hygiene. Be careful using accounts that are logged in on multiple devices, like the unlocked family iPad on the coffee table that has your iMessage logged in. Are your iMessage or WhatsApp accounts logged in on a computer that someone else has access to? Ensuring you log out of shared devices can help prevent any issues.

Use "two-factor" on your accounts, especially critical accounts like e-mail that hold the keys to most other services you use. This means that after you log in to a service, it will request either via a text message, app message, or physical token a second form of confirmation that this is indeed you. This can be turned on in your privacy settings and is one of the most important things you can do to thwart entry to your accounts if someone gets ahold of your password.

Avoiding Open Phone Lines

Not everyone is going to go out and buy burner phones so they can organize or find an abortion in a post-*Roe* America, and sometimes you just have to work with the phone options you have. That's fine, as long as you are working with end-to-end encrypted calls.

This matters because of something called "third-party doctrine," which is the basis of legal authority for institutions to request information from your phone company or any other third party to whom you have given your data. Phone companies typically respond to subpoena requests and give a variety of rich and unfortunately detailed information about the calls, texts, and location information given to their service. This is why, when possible, we opt for communication methods and technologies that do not keep this kind of enriched information.

The Electronic Frontier Foundation offers many tips regarding making secure encrypted voice calls in their Surveillance Self-Defense tool kit, which can be accessed at https://ssd.eff.org. The most important advice they offer is a reminder that most of our most common calls aren't nearly as private as we think they are. After all, these companies will be obligated to respond to government requests like wiretaps or subpoena.

Beware! Most popular VoIP [voice over Internet protocol] providers, such as Skype and Google Hangouts, offer transport encryption so that eavesdroppers cannot listen in, but *the providers themselves are still potentially able to listen in.* Depending on your threat model, this may or may not be a problem.

including photos—if you do this.

2) *Lock down your privacy settings.* If you are using your real account to join groups and post messages, make sure that all your Facebook privacy settings are locked down. Click on "Settings" in the right-hand drop-down menu, then on "Privacy" in the left column on the next page. Change your settings to make sure that only your friends can see your friends list, so no one can contact your friends or family to tell them about your activities. Then go to "Manage Profile" and make sure your e-mail, phone number, and any other identifying information like family members or schools attended is only available to friends. Make your photos private so they cannot be used by others. Remove your workplace if necessary to prevent anyone from trying to contact your employer. Make sure all posts on your page are set to "Friends" rather than "Public." And finally, double-check and see what your page looks like to someone you haven't friended. You can do that by clicking on the three dots beneath your cover photo and hitting "View as."

3) *If asking for money, consider a passthrough account or a throwaway account.* Many people are using Facebook groups to try to crowdsource expenses ranging from emergency contraception to the procedure itself. If you are going to attempt to crowdsource funding (something that wouldn't need to happen at all in a just world), consider reaching out to someone you trust to act as the go-between to protect your own privacy. If you do it yourself, look for an online banking app that you haven't used before and set up a new account (think Cash App or Venmo rather than your usual PayPal account). If you do use an already existing account, remember that for many people their PayPal is their e-mail, too, which opens you up to possible abuse or unwanted interaction. Meanwhile, if you use your Venmo

account, make sure you turn the transactions to private so your contacts don't see what the money is being used for.

4) *Move it to a more secure forum.* Facebook is a VERY easy place for authorities to access information. If you suspect that your conversation could get you into legal trouble, take it to a secure place like a phone call or text on Signal. And be completely sure you trust the person on the other end.

5) *Delete and leave.* Just like with Reddit, make your post, get the help you need, then delete your post and go. If you used a fake new account, deactivate it. If you used your real account, leave the group afterward. The less of a trail you leave, the better.

6) *Sadly, be prepared for some abuse.* Not content with putting themselves in front of patients trying to access abortion clinics, anti-abortion protesters and abortion opponents have decided to also infiltrate online groups in an effort to coerce people out of abortions there too. This is one of the reasons it is so important to try to lock down all of your privacy settings before posting. If someone begins harassing you online, either on your posts or through direct messages, try to report them and ignore them. You don't owe anyone your reasons or your attention.

How to Organize with Others in a Secure Environment

Securing your own electronic footprint and communications is one thing. But what if you want to work with others, either across state lines or international lines? That means making sure everyone follows the same security protocols, and only working with people you are certain are doing it, and who have similar goals as you do.

At *A Womb of One's Own*, the writer refers to this secure and vetted group as a "network of trust." She says:

What is a "network of trust"? Put simply, this is a group of women who want to help each other to ensure that people in their group of friends will be able to make reproductive decisions regardless of legal restrictions.

If you already know your friends to be pro-choice, you may believe it would be easy to build these networks. However, even pro-choice people can sometimes be hesitant to break the law in order to support the cause ... It is important to only allow people into your networks of trust that you believe will keep your secrets safe. While the vast majority of what you will be doing is legal, allowing people into your networks of trust who are not, themselves, trustworthy can create a host of problems.[72]

A "network of trust" isn't just for activities around self-managed abortion care or the medical side of abortion, but it is also imperative if you plan to do any sort of organizing around abortion access post-*Roe*. Being positive that you can trust everyone in your network is just as important when it comes to actions that are completely legal, since allowing someone into your network who isn't trustworthy doesn't just add to the potential legal consequences but can create a dangerous and volatile activist environment too.

Protection from Anti-Abortion Infiltration

Perhaps the most well-known recent incident of letting someone into a network of trust, only to have it abused, is the multiyear infiltration of David Daleiden, the anti-abortion activist who pretended to be a "tissue procurement" professional in order to get access to meetings and events with abortion providers across the country. His edited videos obtained while secretly recording conversations with medical providers—conversations in which Daleiden himself often asked leading questions in an effort to try to egg providers into potentially breaking laws—are a more egregious example of how abortion opponents can infiltrate even the most secure environments.

But for every Daleiden there are many other activists trying to make other inroads into your network of trust—from sending e-mails asking questions in the hopes you might offer advice that is illegal to interacting with you on social media in order to move further into your group of activists. As abortion becomes more restricted, vetting the people you let into your network will become even more vital.

Stay Secure Online

This should be a given, but always be extremely careful of anything you say in e-mail, even if the person sending the e-mail is someone you know. E-mail accounts can be hacked, or someone could even create an e-mail almost identical to—but not quite—the address of the friend in question. We often see what we expect to see, so always play it safe. This is especially important if you or others in your network have public e-mail addresses associated with your work as activists. You can absolutely never be too cautious online.

It is just as important to be vigilant on social media sites. If you plan on posting any information about your activities on Facebook, be absolutely certain that you know every person you allow to be your friend. It is not uncommon for people to set up fake accounts in order to infiltrate a friend circle of people they may see as political enemies, and far too often people will accept friend requests of strangers simply because they have a number of friends in common already. If you have not physically met the person, consider checking in with one of your common friends to ensure they know the person in real life. If it turns out none of your mutual friends know where the person came from, either, there is a pretty good chance you are dealing with a fake account trying to get access to your network.

Vetting Your Contacts

If you have decided to start a new organization—a practical support group for those seeking terminations, a new political action group, or an escorting team at a new clinic or an EC delivery service—you are going to need other volunteers to help you. Here are a few tips for making sure the people you bring on aren't actually trying to sabotage your efforts.

First, the easiest way to make sure your network is safe is to use people you already know and trust. Next, get word-of-mouth recommendations. Expand your current network to a friends-of-friends basis. Again, these should be people that your first volunteers already trust and are prepared to vouch for. Finally, if you do end up expanding to new volunteers who aren't firsthand acquaintances, be sure to vet their Internet presence. A person willing to work in reproductive rights or justice is highly unlikely to have no history whatsoever. Do a Google search, ask if they have social media accounts you can examine. And yes, if necessary, say no to them. It is always better to have too few volunteers doing the work than to have someone in your organization who may be trying to bring it down from the inside.

Protecting Yourself When the Worst Happens

Let's be honest—try as hard as you might, bad stuff still happens. Maybe despite all of your security and all of your vetting, you did end up with an abortion opponent in your personal network. It could have been that coworker from your last job that you stayed in touch with but never talked politics with, or maybe that one cousin who always sends you chain e-mails about angel prayers. Whatever happened, now you've realized that the protesters outside the clinic you are defending are now calling you by your first and last name, or maybe your new boss is getting harassing phone calls demanding you be fired. How do you cope?

Hopefully, before it gets to this point, you have already put some precautions in place to protect your personal information. If you have registered websites, consider paying additional fees to block your name and contact information from being published. If you do register without privacy, considering using a PO Box and setting up a Google voice number for registration in order to avoid giving away your home address.

Your home address and phone number are often stored online and can come up in search engines, too. To remove them, you can go to websites like Spokeo (http://www.spokeo.com/opt_out/new) or Whitepages (https://support.whitepages.com/hc/en-us/articles/115010106908-How-do-I-edit-or-remove-a-personal-listing-) and follow their instructions for opting out. There are also services that can do this for a fee, like DeleteMe or PrivacyDuck.

When it comes to keeping your address private, the most important thing to do is pay attention to your social media. Don't take photos of your home, especially if it shows an address, and be careful about how much identifying information is out there on Facebook, Instagram, or Twitter that could give away your neighborhood simply based on local restaurants or businesses you frequent. Always turn off geotagging to eliminate extra metadata on your photos or check-ins, and be cognizant about putting up things like routes from runs on Runkeeper or other fitness apps that could easily give away your home address.

Also make sure that your employer information is hidden. As more people are networking professionally using LinkedIn, that can be an easy way for someone to find out your current employer, so consider that when thinking about what information you want online. Consider removing your employer information from your Facebook profile, too.

Of course none of this matters if your employer info can be easily accessed though a news search. If there are professional press releases in trade publications or elsewhere, removing your Internet footprint may be far more work than you can accomplish on your own. Take the precautions you can, but don't beat yourself up if you can't do it all.

Dealing with a Cyberattack

Finally, sometimes it isn't just you getting attacked, it's your entire organization. Abortion opponents have allegedly already executed cyberattacks on large reproductive rights organizations. In 2015 an anti-abortion hacker claimed responsibility for a security breech on the Planned Parenthood website, obtaining e-mail addresses and other Planned Parenthood databases.[73] The National Network of Abortion Funds was attacked a year later, with a distributed denial of service attack (DDOS) that shut down its abortion Bowl-a-Thon fund-raiser after attempting to create billions of dollars in fake donations. The hackers also accessed donor e-mails, sending spoofed anti-abortion e-mails with racist language to the real abortion fund donors.[74]

So what should you do to prepare for a potential cyberattack? Most "attacks" result from credentials, or log-in information to the services you use, being disclosed in public breaches of other services. This is why it's important to use long passwords, passwords that differ from each other in case one service you use is compromised, and a two-factor method to ensure that even your password is not enough to access your information.

The first thing to do for any web presence is have an emergency plan that includes a backup of your website, in case you need to revert because hackers put up their own site or inserted inappropriate images into yours. Make sure to back up any information in your databases frequently as well, so a potential wipe won't be as devastating.

Be sure to have all of the information you need to contact your web host immediately in order to get the site fixed—whether it requires taking it offline until it can be restored or even longer to see how intense any breach might be. It's also highly recommended to use an online protection service that can help filter the fake traffic meant to crash your site by overwhelming it with "users" (i.e., a distributed denial of service attack). Many of these services are available for cheap or free for nonprofits or individual users. Some of the ones available for nonprofits include Cloudflare and Google Shield.

If everyone in your organization uses e-mail addresses hosted on the domain, be sure that they have alternate addresses they can use until it can be determined that the original addresses weren't compromised. Also, have a game plan for how to connect with each other to alert all of the volunteers about the hack, especially if you are worried that your electronic communication may no longer be safe.

Why Hard Copies Matter

Finally, remember to keep physical copies of information that you will use on a regular basis, rather than relying solely on the Internet, your computer, or your phone. Viruses can wipe out hard drives.

Your phone could get confiscated. Websites can get hacked. If you have procedures, resource lists, maps and addresses, or other info you use regularly, consider making hard copies and keeping them somewhere safe. Or even take notes here, in this book.

Less than a hundred years ago, it was a crime in the United States to publicize information about abortion or birth control. In Ireland, it was illegal until 2018 to offer public information about abortion services outside the country—only doctors could do so, and only to their patients.

Will the US make publishing and accessing abortion information a crime if abortion itself becomes illegal? The idea seems very unlikely. But that doesn't mean that an anti-abortion administration couldn't find ways to make that information less available through financial coercion of Internet providers or restrictions on content allowed in publicly funded institutions like libraries, public university computer labs, or wireless networks in nonprofit agencies. And even if the government does keep its hands off of abortion information access, we can't be certain that anti-abortion tech activists won't continue their cyberattacks on websites with abortion content.

So, just to be safe, when in doubt, print it out.

Chapter 10 Worksheet
Cleaning Up Your Data Trail

Giving your phone an electronic cleansing is just a good idea in general, but especially when you are a person of reproductive age who wants to keep their privacy secure. Maybe period app tracking is a *Handmaid's Tale* sort of dystopian scenario, but it's just as important to keep your information private from third-party interests as it is from the government. Here are some quick tips to make sure your phone is keeping you safe.

1) *Do an apps check-in.* If you are on a smartphone of any kind, check to see what all is lurking on your phone. Go to your settings and run through your full list. You may be surprised by all the things you downloaded a long time ago and totally forgot about (Word Swipe, I'm looking at you). Lots of apps resell your data, so if you don't use it, toss it.

2) *Watch your location settings.* You don't need your apps to know where you are all the time. Go to your privacy settings and check "Location Services." Then scroll down and see exactly what apps are using your location and decide whether they really need to know. While you are in there, if you are on an iPhone tap "System Services" and scroll down to "Location Based Apple Ads" and turn that off too.

3) *Delete your advertising key ID.* Think of it like a "clear all cookies" for your phone. Go to "Advertising" and tap "Reset Advertising Identifier" to get a clean slate.

4) *Take a look at your "Health."* If you are on an iPhone, some of your health details are already being tracked just via normal activity—like how many steps you take a day. Maybe you don't want that anymore (or maybe you started tracking your menstrual cycles in there once and now wish you hadn't) and it's time to wipe that out? Go to your health settings and click "Delete All Data From 'Health'" for a fresh start.

5) *If you want a period tracker, find one that doesn't sell your data.* According to a Consumer Report Digest investigation in January 2020,[75] five of the major period trackers—BabyCenter, Clue, Flo, My Calendar, and Ovia—were all sharing user information with third parties, usually data brokers who could use

the info for advertising and marketing purposes. Clue and Flo have both started providing additional steps to opt out, but for the most private and secure tracker app try Euki App from Women Help Women. The downside: because it doesn't store user data, it doesn't have a predictive function like the others do.

6) *Turn off your location (and your AirDrop) if you go to a health clinic.* Besides the fact that it makes good privacy sense, anti-abortion activists have been known to geofence (targeting mobile ads to certain locations) abortion and reproductive health clinics, sending patients ads for crisis pregnancy centers or other anti-abortion groups while patients are trying to access care. Meanwhile, an open AirDrop can be used to send links, files, and pictures straight to a person's phone. For your own privacy (and safety), always make sure your AirDrop is set to "Contacts Only."

Permissions

Abortion Desert Image (page 14): Cartwright AF, Karunaratne M, Barr-Walker J, Johns NE, Upadhyay UD. Identifying National Availability of Abortion Care and Distance From Major US Cities: Systematic Online Search. *J Med Internet Res* 2018;20(5):e186 DOI: 10.2196/jmir.9717 PMID: 29759954

Post-Roe desert (page 14)—Derivative, Robin Marty

How to use birth control pills as emergency contraception (page 45–46) from *A Womb of One's Own*, https://wombofonesown.word-press.com. Reprinted with permission.

Infographics on herbal abortion remedies designed and used by Emily Likins-Ehlers, full spectrum doula, for client support. Reprinted with permission.

Instructions for finding abortion pills (page 115–116) from www.Abortionpillinfo.org. Reprinted with permission.

Information and images on how to induce a miscarriage with medications (page 157–161 on) from Women Help Women, Self-Managed Abortion: Safe and Supported, https://womenhelp.org/en/page/408/how-should-I-take-the-pills; https://womenhelp.org/en/page/623/how-to-use-misoprostol-for-abortion-graphic-instructions; https://consult.womenhelp.org/en/page/417/what-to-do-in-%20case-of-emergency Reprinted with permission.

Del Em image (page 187) from Women's Health Specialists, www. womenshealthspecialists.org/self-help/menstrual-extraction/. Reprinted with permission.

How to perform a menstrual extraction (page 188–190) from the Skeptic Files Message board, originally from *Womenpower—Do It Yourself Abortion—Time's Up!*, http://www.skepticfiles.org/atheist2/ selfabor.htm. Reprinted with permission.

How to perform a manual vacuum aspiration (page 191–195) from Médecins Sans Frontières, https://medicalguidelines.msf.org/viewport/EONC/english/9-5-manual-vacuum-aspiration-mva-20316948. html. Reprinted with permission.

Abortion tools picture (page 194) courtesy of author.

Notes

1 Arit John, "Arizona GOPer Resigns After Calling for Forced Sterilization of Women on Medicaid," *Atlantic*, September 15, 2014, https://www.theatlantic.com/politics/archive/2014/09/arizona-goper-resigns-after-calling-for-forced-sterilization-of-women-on-medicaid/380191/.

2 "Henry Hyde Quotes," AZ Quotes, https://www.azquotes.com/author/29083-Henry_Hyde.

3 Sarah Torre, "Hyde Amendment Turns 40: More Than 2 Million Lives Saved," *Daily Signal*, October 5, 2016, https://www.dailysignal.com/2016/10/05/hyde-amendment-turns-40-more-than-2-million-lives-saved/.

4 Michael J. New, "Hyde @ 40: Analyzing the Impact of the Hyde Amendment," Charlotte Lozier Institute, September 27, 2016, https://lozierinstitute.org/hydeat40/.

5 Michelle Garcia, "In Many States the End of Roe v. Wade Is Already Here," Vox.com, July 9, 2018, https://www.vox.com/2018/7/3/17526222/abortion-states-access-roe-v-wade-kennedy.

6 Elizabeth Nash et al., "State Policy Trends 2019: A Wave of Abortion Bans, But Some States Are Fighting Back," Guttmacher Institute, De-cember 10, 2019, https://www.guttmacher.org/article/2019/12/state-policy-trends-2019-wave-abortion-bans-some-states-are-fighting-back.

7 Robin Marty, "The Long Road to a Safe and Legal Abortion," *Slate*, October 20, 2014, https://slate.com/human-interest/2014/10/abortion-clinic-crisis-women-of-texas-could-have-to-drive-up-to-600-miles-to-end-a-pregnancy.html.

8 "Abortion in Latin America and the Caribbean," Guttmacher Institute, March 2018, https://www.guttmacher.org/fact-sheet/abortion-latin-america-and-caribbean.

9 "North Carolina Motorcycle Abortion Bill Passes State House," *Huffington Post*, July 11, 2013, https://www.huffingtonpost.com/2013/07/11/north-carolina-motorcycle-abortion_n_3582006.html.

10 "What If Roe Fell," Center for Reproductive Rights, accessed August 1, 2018, https://www.reproductiverights.org/what-if-roe-fell.

11   Marlene Gerber Fried, "The Hyde Amendment: 30 Years of Violating
      Women's Rights," Center for American Progress, October 6, 2006, https://
      www.americanprogress.org/issues/women/news/2006/10/06/2243/the-hyde-
      amendment-30-years-of-violating-womens-rights/.

12   "Which Kind of Emergency Contraception Should I Use?," Planned
      Parenthood, accessed August 27, 2018, https://www.plannedparenthood.org/
      learn/morning-after-pill-emergency-contraception/which-kind-emergency-
      contraception-should-i-use.

13   "Unintended Pregnancy in the United States," Guttmacher Institute, September
      2016, https://www.guttmacher.org/fact-sheet/unintended-pregnancy-united-
      states.

14   "Beyond the Beltway," Power to Decide, August 2018, https://powertodecide.
      org/system/files/resources/primary-download/extended-supply-contraception.
      pdf.

15   Jane Doe, *A Womb of One's Own*, June 30, 2014, accessed August 11, 2018, https://
      wombofonesown.wordpress.com/2014/06/30/a-womb-of-ones-own-complete-text-
      basic-edition/.

16   "ACOG Practice Bulletin," American College of Obstetricians and
      Gynecologists, November 2017, https://www.acog.org/Clinical-Guidance-and-
      Publications/Practice-Bulletins/Committee-on-Practice-Bulletins-Gynecology/
      Long-Acting-Reversible-Contraception-Implants-and-Intrauterine-Devices.

17   Ariana Eunjung Cha, "New Federally Funded Clinics Emphasize Absti-
      nence, Natural Family Planning," *Washington Post*, July 29, 2019, https://
      www.washingtonpost.com/health/2019/07/22/new-federally-funded-clinics-
      california-emphasize-abstinence-natural-family-planning/.

18   Jenna Birch, "Are Birth Control Apps an Effective Form of Contracep-tion?,"
      Huffington Post, June 17, 2019, https://www.huffpost.com/entry/fertility-
      tracking-apps-birth-control_l_5d0117bee4b0dc17ef02a10a.

19   Andrea Swartzendruber, Riley J. Steiner, and Anna Newton-Levinson,
      "Contraceptive Information on Pregnancy Center Websites: A Statewide
      Content Analysis," *Contraception*, April 24, 2018, https://pubmed.ncbi.nlm.
      nih.gov/29702081/.

20   Amanda Marcotte, "Virginia Crisis Pregnancy Centers Caught Lying About
      Abortion and *Contraception*," Slate, August 9, 2013, https://slate.com/human-
      interest/2013/08/naral-virginia-catches-crisis-pregnancy-centers-lying-about-
      abortion-and-contraception.html.

21   Safe and Sound for Women Pricing, Las Vegas, NV, accessed September 16, 2018, http://www.safeandsoundforwomen.com/you-should-know/.

22   Ronnie Cohen, "Denial of Abortion Leads to Economic Hardship for Low-Income Women," Reuters, January 18, 2018, https://www.reuters.com/article/us-health-abortion-hardship/denial-of-abortion-leads-to-economic-hardship-for-low-income-women-idUSKBN1F731Z.

23   Hannah Smothers, "People Are Urging Women to Start Saving an Emergency Abortion Fund," *Cosmopolitan*, November 10, 2016, https://www.cosmopolitan.com/sex-love/a8274910/people-are-urging-women-to-start-saving-an-emergency-abortion-fund/.

24   Perry Stein, "Proposed Zoning Changes Would Restrict Abortion Clinics in Manassas," *Washington Post*, April 27, 2015, https://www.washingtonpost.com/local/virginia-politics/proposed-zoning-changes-would-restrict-abortion-clinics-in-manassas/2015/04/27/8a28df92-ece9-11e4-8666-a1d756d0218e_story.html?utm_term=.8aae66c2bd2a.

25   "'It Was Just One Thing After Another': An Abortion Provider on His Four-Month Ordeal to Reopen the Only Clinic in Northern Alabama," *Slate*, October 28, 2014, http://www.slate.com/articles/double_x/doublex/2014/10/dalton_johnson_on_reopening_an_abortion_clinic_in_alabama.html.

26   "Whole Woman's Health Officially Announces South Bend Abortion Clinic Plans," WNDU News, October 30, 2017, https://www.wndu.com/content/news/Whole-Womans-Health-officially-announces-South-Bend-abortion-clinic-plans-454149003.html.

27   Jeff Parrot, "South Bend Council Allows Anti-Abortion Group to Open Site Next to Proposed Abortion Clinic," *South Bend Tribune*, April 24, 2018, https://www.southbendtribune.com/news/local/south-bend-council-allows-anti-abortion-group-to-open-site/article_f516f3b8-3e60-5bd9-9889-3b6ee69e606e.html.

28   "Fact Sheet: Science of Fetal Pain," Charlotte Lozier Institute, February 19, 2020, https://lozierinstitute.org/fact-sheet-science-of-fetal-pain/.

29   Sara G. Miller, "Do Fetuses Feel Pain? What the Science Says," Live Science, May 17, 2016, https://www.livescience.com/54774-fetal-pain-anesthesia.html.

30   "Tips on Writing a Letter to the Editor," ACLU, accessed October 22, 2020, https://www.aclu.org/other/tips-writing-letter-editor.

31   Mariella Mosthof, "John Oliver's Segment About Crisis Pregnancy Centers on 'Last Week Tonight' Sheds Light on Their Misleading Tactics," *Romper*,

April 8, 2018, https://www.romper.com/p/john-olivers-segment-about-crisis-pregnancy-centers-on-last-week-tonight-sheds-light-on-their-misleading-tactics-8728576.

32   "Characteristics of U.S. Abortion Patients in 2014 and Changes Since 2008," Guttmacher Institute, May 2016, https://www.guttmacher.org/report/characteristics-us-abortion-patients-2014.

33   "I'm an Abortion Doula—Here's What I Do and See During a Typical Shift," Self, June 1, 2017, https://www.self.com/story/abortion-doula.

34   Willie Parker, MD, "Dr. Willie Parker: The South Is 'Ground Zero' in the Abortion Fight," *Glamour*, April 5, 2018, https://www.glamour.com/story/dr-willie-parker-the-south-is-ground-zero-in-the-abortion-access-fight.

35   Jody Steinauer, "Want to Protect the Right to Abortion? Train More People to Perform Them," *New York Times*, August 29, 2018, https://www.nytimes.com/2018/08/29/opinion/abortion-provider-training-roe.html.

36   "Reproductive Justice," SisterSong.net, accessed September 4, 2018, https://www.sistersong.net/reproductive-justice/.

37   Emily Stewart, "How to Be a Good White Ally, According to Activists," Vox.com, June 2, 2020, https://www.vox.com/2020/6/2/21278123/being-an-ally-racism-george-floyd-protests-white-people.

38   Philip Bump, "Trump Celebrates Winning 52 Percent of Women in 2016—Which Is Only How He Did Among Whites," *Washington Post*, March 10, 2018, https://www.washingtonpost.com/news/politics/wp/2018/03/10/trump-celebrates-winning-52-percent-of-women-in-2016-which-is-only-how-he-did-among-whites/?utm_term=.3c4c64110e5a.

39   Tamar Auber, "Protesters Pound on Doors of Supreme Court: 'Kavanaugh Has Hot to Ho,'" Mediaite.com, October 6, 2018, https://www.mediaite.com/tv/protesters-pound-on-doors-of-supreme-court-kavanaugh-has-got-to-go/.

40   Mark Joseph Stern, "Georgia Just Criminalized Abortion. Women Who Terminate Their Pregnancies Would Receive Life in Prison," , Slate, May 7, 2019, https://slate.com/news-and-politics/2019/05/hb-481-georgia-law-criminalizes-abortion-subjects-women-to-life-in-prison.html.

41   Erin Matson, "When It Comes to Abortion Rights, Civil Disobedience Could Be the Only Option," *Teen Vogue*, August 16, 2018, https://www.teenvogue.com/story/when-it-comes-to-abortion-rights-civil-disobedience-could-be-the-only-option.

42   David DeKok, "Mom Ann Whalen Sentenced to Prison for Giving Daughter Abortion Pills," Reuters, September 6, 2014, https://www.huffingtonpost.com/2014/09/07/ann-whalen-abortion-daughter_n_5777120.html.

43   Tara Culp-Ressler, "Over 60 Pro-Choice Activists Arrested for Protesting North Carolina's Radical Abortion Restrictions," ThinkProgress, July 9, 2013, https://thinkprogress.org/over-60-pro-choice-activists-arrested-for-protesting-north-carolinas-radical-abortion-restrictions-cc00133de6d3/.

44   "Rachel Sadon, "Kavanaugh Confirmed Amidst Day of Protests and More Than 150 Arrests in D.C.," DCist, October 6, 2018, https://dcist.com/story/18/10/06/kavanaugh-confirmation-protests/.

45   Anatol Magdziarz and Marc Santora, "Women Converge on Warsaw, Heightening Poland's Largest Protests in Decades," New York Times, October 30, 2020, https://www.nytimes.com/2020/10/30/world/europe/poland-abortion-women-protests.html.

46   H. S. Seo, "125 Women Take 'Abortion Pill' in Protest of Anti-Abortion Law," Korea BizWire, August 27, 2018, http://koreabizwire.com/125-women-take-abortion-pill-in-protest-of-anti-abortion-law/123240.

47   Molly Redden, "New Website Offers US Women Help to Perform Their Own Abortions," Guardian, April 27, 2017, https://www.theguardian.com/world/2017/apr/27/abortion-website-women-help-women.

48   "Abortifacient Herbs," Sister Zeus, accessed August 11, 2018, http://www.sisterzeus.com/Abortif.htm.

49   Kimberly Lawson, "Federal Judge Rules You Can Get the Abortion Pill Through the Mail During the Pandemic," Courier News Room, July, 14, 2020, https://couriernewsroom.com/2020/07/14/federal-judge-rules-you-can-get-the-abortion-pill-through-the-mail-during-the-pandemic/.

50   Julia Belluz, "Abortions by Mail; the FDA Is Going After Online Pill Pro-viders," Vox.com, March 12, 2019, https://www.vox.com/2019/3/12/18260699/misoprostol-mifepristone-medical-abortion.

51   Department of Justice, US Attorney's Office, Western District of Wisconsin, "New York Woman Sentenced for Selling Abortion-Inducing Pills Illegally Smuggled into US," U.S. Food and Drug Administration, July 10, 2020, https://www.fda.gov/inspections-compliance-enforcement-and-criminal-investigations/press-releases/new-york-woman-sentenced-selling-abortion-inducing-pills-illegally-smuggled-us.

52 David Brennan, "Woman Dies After Using Parsley to Induce Miscarriage, First Death Since Argentina Senate Rejected Abortion Bill," *Newsweek*, August 15, 2018, https://www.newsweek.com/woman-dies-after-using-parsley-induce-miscarriage-first-death-argentina-1073864.

53 Arielle Swernoff, "How to Give Yourself an Abortion," Jewish Currents, January 9, 2020, https://jewishcurrents.org/how-to-give-yourself-an-abortion/.

54 Abigail R. A. Aiken et al., "Self Reported Outcomes and Adverse Events After Medical Abortion through Online Telemedicine: Population Based Study in the Republic of Ireland and Northern Ireland," *BMJ*, May 16, 2017, https://www.bmj.com/content/357/bmj.j2011.

55 *When Self-Induced Abortion Is a Crime: Laws That Put Women at Risk*, National Institute for Reproductive Health, June 2017, https://www.nirhealth.org/wp-content/uploads/2017/06/Self-Abortion-White-Paper-Final.pdf.

56 DeKok, "Mom Ann Whalen Sentenced."

57 "Roe's Unfinished Promise: Decriminalizing Abortion Once and for All," SIA Legal Team, accessed August 8, 2018, https://www.sialegalteam.org/roes-unfinished-promise.

58 Nellie Gilles, Sarah Kramer, and Joe Richman, "Before 'Roe v. Wade,' the Women of 'Jane' Provided Abortions for the Women of Chicago," NPR, January 19, 2018, https://www.npr.org/2018/01/19/578620266/before-roe-v-wade-the-women-of-jane-provided-abortions-for-the-women-of-chicago.

59 Kate Manning, "Leeches, Lye and Spanish Fly," *New York Times*, January 21, 2013, https://www.nytimes.com/2013/01/22/opinion/leeches-lye-and-spanish-fly.html.

60 Daniella Silva, "Anna Yocca, Tennessee Woman in Coat-Hanger Attempted Abortion Case, Released from Jail a Year Later," NBC News, January 11, 2017, https://www.nbcnews.com/news/us-news/anna-yocca-tennessee-woman-coat-hanger-attempted-abortion-case-released-n705416.

61 S. A. Miller, "Activists Perform Watermelon Abortion at Liberal Convention: 'Folks Feel OK Afterward," *Washington Times*, July 12, 2019, https://www.washingtontimes.com/news/2019/jul/12/activists-perform-watermelon-abortion-netroots-nat/.

62 Marie Solis, "I Learned How to Do an Abortion on a Papaya," *VICE News*, July 24, 2019, https://www.vice.com/en_us/article/3k334w/how-to-do-an-abortion-with-manual-vacuum-aspiration-papaya-workshop.

63 "Building a Del Em," *Reproductive Right Blog*, accessed August 11, 2010, http://the-reproductive-right.blogspot.com/p/building-del-em.html.

64 Emily Bazelon, "A Mother in Jail for Helping Her Daughter Have an Abortion," *New York Times Magazine*, September 22, 2014, https://www.nytimes.com/2014/09/22/magazine/a-mother-in-jail-for-helping-her-daughter-have-an-abortion.html.

65 Lisa Ryan, "How to Plan an Abortion in the Surveillance State," *Cut*, January 25, 2017, https://www.thecut.com/2017/01/how-to-safely-research-and-learn-about-abortion.html.

66 "What to Do If Your Phone Is Seized by the Police," ACLU Freedom of the Press Foundation, June 27, 2018, accessed August 11, 2018, https://freedom.press/training/mobile-security-for-activists-and-journalists/.

67 Mark Yates, "Three Reasons to Never Use Fingerprint Locks on Phones," AVG Signal, July 12, 2016, https://www.avg.com/en/signal/3-reasons-to-never-use-fingerprint-locks.

68 "Surveillance Self-Defense: Communicating with Others," Electronic Frontier Foundation, accessed August 11, 2018, https://ssd.eff.org/en/module/communicating-others.

69 Russell Brandom, "Police Are Using DNA Testing to Track Down a Fetus's Mother," *Verge*, May 10, 2018, https://www.theverge.com/2018/5/10/17340666/dna-testing-georgia-fetus-codis-abortion-genetics-investigation.

70 Ryan Phillips, "Infant Death Case Heading Back to Grand Jury," Starkville Daily News, May 9, 2019, https://www.starkvilledailynews.com/infant-death-case-heading-back-to-grand-jury/article_cf99bcb0-71cc-11e9-963a-eb5dc5052c92.html.

71 Molly Redden, "Purvi Patel Has 20-Year Sentence for Inducing Her Own Abortion Reduced," Guardian, July 22, 2016, https://www.theguardian.com/us-news/2016/jul/22/purvi-patel-abortion-sentence-reduced.

72 *A Womb of One's Own.*

73 Theodore Schleifer, "Anti-Abortion Group Claims Credit for Planned Parenthood Hacking," CNN, July 27, 2015, https://www.cnn.com/2015/07/27/politics/planned-parenthood-hacked/index.html.

74   Sara Ashley O'Brien, "Abortion Funds Band Together to Sue Cyberattackers," CNN, March 29, 2018, https://money.cnn.com/2018/03/29/technology/abortion-fundraiser-cyberattack-lawsuit/index.html.

75   Donna Rosato, "What Your Period Tracker App Knows About You," Consumer Reports, January 28, 2020, https://www.consumerreports.org/health-privacy/what-your-period-tracker-app-knows-about-you/.

Index

AAF. *see* Abortion Access Force (AAF)

AASN. *see* Arkansas Abortion Support Network (AASN) (Little Rock)

"abortifacient," 35

abortion. *see also* abortion access; abortion bans; abortion clinics; abortion funds/funding; abortion opponents; abortion rights; pre-Roe ban on abortion
  at-home, preparing for, 178–181
  "average" budget, 57–58
  D&C, 184, 185
  decision of having, 13
  getting support for, 59–62
  herbal, 153–154, 155–161
  Hyde opposition to, 1
  illegal, 9–10, 71–76, 149
  in Latin America and Caribbean, 10
  number of people with, 90
  performed by non-doctors, 199–200
  performed by non-Planned Parenthood clinics, 29
  pre-Roe, 185–186
  rape and, 2
  restrictions, protesting, 147–149
  "safe," 10
  within the state, 6, 15–28
  "taxpayer funded abortion," 79–80
  United States Supreme Court ruling on, 1

abortion access
  as civil rights issue, 139
  in Delaware, 17
  federal agencies and blocking of, 163–165
  fighting to protect locally, 66
  Michigan as highly restricted, 20
  New York funding for, 68–69
  NNAF membership and, 84
  in northern Alabama, 67
  Ohio and block of, 24
  overturn of laws and, 146
  in Pennsylvania, 25
  restrictions of, 2
  South Korean women and, 149
  training abortion providers to maintain, 113–114

Abortion Access Force (AAF), 89–90, 122–123

abortion assistance, finding, 196–198

abortion bans
  Alabama's legislature passing, 15
  in Arkansas, 16
  Georgia state legislature in 2019, 141–142
  Ireland under, 9
  medication, 4
  overturn of Roe and, 140
  pre-Roe, in Louisiana, 19
  South Korean women protesting, 149
  in Texas, 26
  victim of, in Argentina, 156

abortion Bowl-a-Thon fund-raiser, 220

Abortion Care Network, 29

abortion clinics, 9. *see also* clinic escorts
  in California, 16
  in Delaware, 17
  finding the right provider and information, 31–32
  in Louisville Kentucky, 19
  in Missouri, 21–22
  in Montana, 22
  in New Mexico, 23
  in Ohio, 24, 80
  in Oregon, 24
  in South Dakota, 7
  Supreme Court ruling and difficulties for, 6, 7
  in Wyoming, 28

Abortion Conversation Project, 90, 91

"abortion deserts," map of, 13

The Abortion Diary, 90

abortion doulas, 105–106, 174

abortion funds/funding
  donating gas cards, restaurant cards, and other gifts, 96–97
  donating miles and hotel points, 97–98
  local, to contact an escort, 117–118
  personal emergency, setting up, 54–58
  state and regional funds, 94–95
  vs, practical support group, 98, 99
  ways of donating, 95–96